For the
Living
of
These Days

David L. Petty

WESTBOW
P R E S S®
A DIVISION OF THOMAS NELSON
& ZONDERVAN

WestBow Press books may be ordered through booksellers or by contacting:

WestBow Press
A Division of Thomas Nelson & Zondervan
1663 Liberty Drive
Bloomington, IN 47403
www.westbowpress.com
1 (866) 928-1240

Because of the dynamic nature of the Internet, any web addresses or links contained in this book may have changed since publication and may no longer be valid. The views expressed in this work are solely those of the author and do not necessarily reflect the views of the publisher, and the publisher hereby disclaims any responsibility for them.

All scripture quotations are taken from the Disciples' Study Bible. Copyright @ 1988 by Holman Bible Publishers. All rights reserved. International copyright secured. Bible text: The Holy Bible, New International Version copyright @ 1973, 1978, 1984 by International Bible Society. All rights reserved. Used with permission of Zondervan Bible Publishers.'

Any people depicted in stock imagery provided by Thinkstock are models, and such images are being used for illustrative purposes only. Certain stock imagery © Thinkstock.

ISBN: 978-1-4908-9882-7 (sc)
ISBN: 978-1-4908-9884-1 (hc)
ISBN: 978-1-4908-9883-4 (e)

Library of Congress Control Number: 2015919462

Print information available on the last page.

WestBow Press rev. date: 02/25/2016

To Mary

Faithful until the end – and beyond.
A mother's love is exceeded only by God's love!

CONTENTS

INTRODUCTION

This story is true; the names herein – all save mine – have been changed for obvious reasons. I retain my name for I need to be responsible for all that I say. I also wish to protect geographical locales and specific organizations.

My intention is to share the remarkable, albeit brief, pilgrimage of a young man on death row. The several roles that he played, given his restricting circumstances, are extraordinary and worthy of sharing.

My book title comes from Harry Emerson Fosdick's great hymn, *God of Grace and God of Glory.* It seemed apropos because my pen-pal and I found that during our 13 years of corresponding, we needed God's power, wisdom and courage "for the living of our days!"

The bulk of this book consists of portions of Joe's letters, reproduced *verbatim* except where changes were demanded for clarity and language deemed inappropriate. While some misspellings are left unchanged and some other punctuations would be preferable, my pen-pal's writing is left unchanged. Errors that he made I liken to a mathematics student who correctly solves a complex problem but gets the wrong answer due to a simple error in arithmetic. Joe's writings were understandable though not always polished; he is to be commended for improvement over time because he worked to that end.

CHAPTER 1

The Beginning

Harry Joseph Prescott was on death-row at a prison in one of our southern states. In mid-1990 he had been charged with, and later convicted of, killing a young woman, the daughter-in-law of a city official in that state. Joe, as he wished to be called, had been locked away for several years when he first wrote to me in late 1999. This is how his story began for me:

"Dear Mr. David Petty,

Hello! My name is Joseph Prescott. I go by Joe. Your name was given to me as someone whom might want to correspond with someone like me. I'm on death-row in _____. So I'm looking for someone who is anti-death penalty and wishes to write to someone like me in this predicament.

At some point the state wishes to kill me. So I'm trying to find some distraction from the monotony and dreariness of this life that I have to endure, until then. Hopefully it won't happen! If you're one of these people who has compassion and some human decency that you could spare me, I'd be able to look forward to the next day." (10- -99).

"So," thought I, "who is this Harry Joseph Prescott? How did he get my name? Shall I become pen-pals with him?"

What was I to do? This was new territory for me. Though I earlier had taught senior college courses at a maximum-security prison in Texas, I had never met a death-row inmate. I wondered if it might be beneficial for both of us if we could correspond for a while. I decided to write back:

"Dear Joe,

Thank you for taking time to write to me, and please say thanks to the person who gave you my name. I am willing to correspond with you periodically, and I hope that it will be mutually beneficial.

You have told me a little about yourself; I will return the favor. For almost 40 years I have claimed Jesus Christ as my Lord and Savior. He is the prime Motivator in my life, for in Him I am experiencing abundant life; and I have His promise of eternal life. My relationship with God, the Father, through His Son, Jesus Christ, has influenced practically all of my life since young adulthood. Whatever human decency and compassion I have comes from this relationship.

I am a retired teacher as is my wife; we have three sons and two daughters-in-law. For several years during my university teaching career, I was privileged to teach several sociology courses at a maximum-security unit of the Texas Department of Corrections.

If we continue to correspond, you can count on me to be truthful and candid with you; in turn, I expect the same from you. When you write again, please explain why you are on death-row." (10-13-99).

After mailing this first letter, I asked myself, "why am I doing this?" I didn't know then, but two possibilities have come to mind through the ensuing 12-13 years.

1. At various times along the way, I recalled Dietrich Bonnhoeffer's *Letters and Papers from Prison*, which I read while studying at seminary in the late 1960s. I thought that maybe one day Joe's and my thoughts and experiences would be interesting and valuable reading for others. We were, after all, sharing our heart-feelings – valuable commodities in our lives!

2. Perhaps my primary reason for telling about these 12 years of Joe's brief life is to have the reader wrestle with this question: what do you think would be the very best end-of-the-story for those criminals who were guilty and convicted of their crime and who served a period of incarceration? Here are some possible answers; do you have another?

- Capital punishment! Get rid of (permanently) this menace to our society, and don't spend our taxes imprisoning such a beast! This solution would seem to aptly describe the vengeful-minded person. What other motives might persuade persons to opt for capital punishment?
- Imprisonment for life without parole (LWOP)! This solution would perhaps come from an anti-death penalty individual who wishes to keep the offender off the streets permanently.
- Imprisonment for a specified period of time with opportunities (chosen or mandated) for the offender to be rehabilitated and then restored to the community. Such rehabilitation would ideally provide needed skills for re-entry to society. Education (academic and vocational) and counseling could bring favorable results for responsible citizenship. Are offenders worthy of such services?
- Probation or parole for a specified period of time with appropriate reparations, community service and the like.

During the years that were to unfold for Joe and me, I had ample time to consider and reconsider my own and society's debates about how to deal with criminal offenders. As with many other social programs, we continue to experiment and change as we search for the best solutions.

While earlier I had interfaced with inmates who were enrolled in my college classes offered behind bars, soon-to-come was another opportunity that would run concurrently with my pen-paling with Joe. In September, 2001, I began to teach Bible classes weekly at a minimum- security unit at the Penitentiary of New Mexico. This program, called Community Bible Study (InPrison), gave me the time to interface with a different set of inmates, sex offenders and other kinds of addicts.

None of these were "lifers" (sentenced for life), so, all things being equal, each would one day be returned to society. Though I was forbidden to ask any about their offense(s), a few would readily offer that information. As I had opportunity to stay in touch with several inmates following their release, I learned of their difficulties of being accepted (graciously or at all) back into the free community.

Rejections were especially grievous for the sex offenders, all of whom are required to register themselves as such in the states to which they return. One man, James, whom I drove to the airport on the day of his release, had an especially-difficult transition. In his native Ohio, as he attempted to align with a local church, he was informally rejected by members as they learned of his background. Cold shoulders, not second chances, were offered by that congregation. He called me periodically to bemoan his situation; and, when we last communicated, this situation had not been resolved.

As I struggled to understand reasons for these impasses, my scientific objectivity kicked in. I was looking at the situations only from my inmate-friends' point of view; society's views are equally important. Society has already been offended (violated) by an individual who has broken one or more of its laws. Society, then, has a right (and responsibility) to ask the offender of his/her future intentions.

Two other considerations are also vital: (1) the current recidivism rate and whether or not the offender is a repeater and (2) whether or not the individual is a sex offender and, more specifically, is s(he) a predator (a pedophile, rapist or the like). High recidivism rates demand that citizens be cautious.

David L. Petty

Two hallmarks of Christianity are repentance (genuine contrition for having done wrong) and forgiveness (to pardon or excuse a wrong). When genuine, these combine to contribute to the doctrine of a "second chance." I invite my readers to join me in this continuing conflict with our law-violators and a proper meting out of justice and mercy for us all.

CHAPTER 2

Joe, the Trusty

As an adjective, the word trusty means trustworthy and reliable. As a noun, the word defines a convict who is given special privileges because of his good behavior.

Many correctional facilities allow trusties certain privileges as payment for certain tasks rendered. Pragmatically, the institution might view this as free (or cheap) labor, while the inmate might see it as an opportunity for a bit more freedom within his confines and/or a relief from boredom.

In any case, my friend Joe decided he'd like to be a trusty. In late 2007, as Joe was recapping the year, he wrote:

> "I started the year out with a goal in mind to convince the prison that it would be a good idea for the prison to allow death row to have its own trustees.* We did some years ago. But we could sure use them. I wrote a letter to the warden putting forth a chart of five reasons why we needed one, and 10 reasons why I would be a

---

* This spelling of the word denotes a person appointed to manage the affairs of a business firm, etc. or a person holding property in trust for another.

good choice. I thought that it might be rejected out of hand, but it met with favoritism. But he was not of sufficient rank to effect change. He passed it up the chain-of-command. A couple of months later I wrote again. Still favorable response, but no change. A couple of months after that the deputy warden was coming around asking opinions of the proposal. I signed up and not long after that, I put a petition together and passed it around the tier asking people to endorse me as the trustee for the tier. I got 17 of 26 signatures, but soon after two other guys were chosen for the jobs. I was really disappointed. I wanted to know why I was overlooked, and honest to God I was told that I had gone about it all wrong (I had gone about it logically). I was flabbergasted that someone would even suggest or repeat such a thing.

In the end it looked as if it was a terribly good thing that I did not get the job. One of those selected was stabbed-to-death by a state prisoner. It was an awful thing to hear. But it made me mad. Made me very angry, Dave. I was trying to get that position and someone does that with no rhyme or reason, and I see them not caring if I was out there or not. Makes me mad to think that someone else would want to do that to me.

The guy that did the killing is now in that super-max prison in Colorado. He had no idea how rough it could be until he got there.

There is talk of filling empty slots for three trustee positions. I have signed up again. I won't be deterred from my goal.

That was the third killing of the year. The first was back in May where a guy was speared with a broom handle. The second was in July where a gang of folks got out of their exercise pens and stabbed someone." (12-6-07).

Less than a year later, Joe's desire to become a trusty materialized. In August, he wrote:

"August was a month of change for us. On the 6th, we were told to pack our stuff because we were moving. This had been in the works for months. Most of the guys were moved off my tier before lunch, but I was one of the last to go. I packed all my stuff in a laundry and garbage bag. It wasn't much, but it was still more than the allowable items. They didn't hassle me about it. I was loaded into a van, driven one building over and off-loaded. They took me inside and put me on an upstairs tier. Only one other time have I been upstairs. The tiers in this building are shorter and there are only 12 guys total. I like the fewer guys, but they are folks I haven't been around for a while or at all. More change!

I stress change because August 10 made 12 years that I have been at ___. Twelve years in one spot and you get used to that familiarity – even in a

9

prison. To be uprooted to some place new takes some getting used to.

The cells are the same, but the shelves had been knocked off the walls years ago. They welded a steel one up for which my TV rests on. A cable antenna wire has been run, but it's a dead wire because it is not hooked to an outside antenna. We missed all of the Olympics and will continue to miss stuff until they solve that problem. They know how consumed by TV some of these guys are and how they act up without that to occupy their time, but they still allow things to go haywire.

The next day, the 7th, I started my first day on the job as a trustee. More change! I had been trying for this position since January, 2007. For whatever reason, I was passed up several times, but I finally got a spot. It's an incredibly easy job. All I do is clean the two shower stalls, 8' X 3', sweeping and mopping the tier, cleaning the concrete tables, the bars and the walls. I move up and down the tier so I take care of the business for the guys. I'm not supposed to do that, but I do clean it up every now and then.

I like the exercise and movement. I break out into a sweat cleaning the showers! But the guys can be a headache; you know what I mean? There are only 11 other guys, but they act like they have multiple personalities. I'm not gonna quit, but

I sure wish I had a different set of prisoners to work with...

Thankfully I do not have to do the cleaning every day. I have a co-worker, Le. He works Sun.-Tues., every alternate Wed., and I work Thur.-Sat. Tomorrow is my Wed. The added work means that I have to make sure to get all other chores done before 4 in the afternoon. I usually try to come out about 5 and lock down at 10. I've worked 13 days so far.

I got a pair of boots and a cap – my trustee garb. I wore my NDGs out and was glad to be able to throw them away once I got the boots. Those things have woke up parts of the soles of my feet I haven't been used to. I wore them and the cap outside. The lieutenant got on to me about the cap because I'm not to wear it outside. I got into a discussion on it being a 'sun visor' and all that. I'm only to wear it when I serve trays as a hair net. Well, serving trays is not part of my trustee job; so I wear it inside to block those bright fluorescent lights." (9-02-08).

After Joe had been working at the trusty job for a month, he gave an update that was indicative of his usual positive attitude:

"The trustee job is going well. It can get boring if I don't pace myself. But I've worked out a routine, and the tier operates around that.

Last week, the ACA folks came in to do an accreditation. The warden sent word that next day that our tier would be rewarded for being so clean with a steak-and-ice cream dinner. That has yet to materialize – or even when it might.

I was surprised at the 'possible' reward because I didn't feel the tier was up to my standard of cleanliness. It's one of the drawbacks to cleaning here that it's hard to get the tier behind me to keep it clean. They don't care, and I can't instill that attitude this late in their life." (10-07-08).

My somewhat limited experience with prison life probably renders my observations somewhat suspect, but I have noted considerable fluidity in the ones in which I have visited or worked. By the term fluid I mean rapid movement and change. For example, in the Level II minimum security facility where I facilitate a Community Bible Study (InPrison) program (for the past 12 years), the turn-over of inmates is quite brisk. While some of this movement is due to inmates being moved about the state, practically all are within four years of release into the community on either probation or parole.

I suspect that one chief reason for fluidity in a maximum-security facility is to keep those inmates off-balance and less able to establish any routine that might adversely affect the unit's operation. Earlier in this chapter, we noted Joe's mention of changing from one unit to another and the frequent turn-over of trusties. He shared another example of change in June, 2009:

"Well, I have become the sole trustee for my tier. My co-worker was fired along with three other guys. Too bold with their movements forced the prison to rein them in. You can't butt heads with the system; you have to work around it. Other tiers have gotten new guys to replace the ones that were fired, but no one seems interested in coming out in my tier. I may be the sole guy for some time to come. It's a huge change from 13 years sedentary, then 3 or 4 days working, and then doing it all the time. Along with my regular writing, reading and working out... It's no wonder I've lost 30 pounds the last two years!" (6-08-09).

Three months later, another change blind-sided Joe:

"I lost my trustee job! It took me a year and a half to get it, and I had it 11 months. I moved a telephone to one of the guys – which was a restricted area at the time. The warden was watching the cameras that day, and he fired me. I've been trying to get the job back. He told me because I admitted that I was in the wrong and that I still wanted the job, that he would consider me in the future to get back out. I had to go 90 days and that ended Friday. I will learn one way or another this week what the deal is. What was a restricted area before no longer is. They changed the rules just after I got fired to let us move into that area to clean it up.

Hopefully I'll get it back because I need the motivation that it provided. I've gotten a bad case of mental and physical lethargy that I want to get rid of. I feel so much better to have the chance to set goals and try to achieve them. I don't do so well with too much idleness." (9-21-09).

Fortunately for him, Joe was re-instated a month later:

"And yes, some good news, as I got my trustee job back. I got fired for passing the phone into a restricted area. Soon after that, the restriction was lifted, but I couldn't just get the job back. I had to go 90 days trouble-free and then reapply. While I was doing that, I convinced some officers to give recommendations to the warden to let me back out. That all worked out because I started again on the 22nd of September.

It's good to get it back because I lost my motivation. I need a challenge. I don't do well with idleness – hence the letter-writing schedule. I had slumped to 12 hours of sleeping each day. Now I've cut that to half. I get up at 5 or 6 to do my reading, writing, workout, whatever. In the afternoon I'm free to do the cleaning without restriction. I can move up and down the tier and not be hassled by the officers. I sweep, mop, clean the showers, tables and food cart, pick up garbage, pass out laundry and a few other things. I get my shower at 10, go to bed at 11 and get up and do it again.

I'm the only trustee so I have to do it 7 days a week. I'd like a co-worker, but no one wants the other slot and even if they did, they wouldn't be eligible. So that leaves me with a lot of motivation. I have to get up early and stay up in order to be able to handle all my personal chores and that of the tier.

This forces me to be structured. The schedule for the letters helps to keep them organized and my days focused on each person that I need to contact. Plus it lets me get some recreational reading done. I hadn't done much all year, but I've done two other books this month.

Lately I've been working on getting some privileges out of the prison for the work. Yesterday I got a radio and a pair of head phones. I have a few other things that I'd like to talk them out of too. A bit of persistence might do the trick." (10-21-09).

During the year 2010, business continued as usual for Joe. He was making the most out of what many would call a dismal existence. I believe that the unusual regimen he developed allowed him to meet each day with optimism and desire to accomplish something meaningful. Indeed, I'm reminded of Brother Lawrence, who believed that washing dishes, pots and pans each day for his order of monks was a way to glorify God. And both remind me of Paul who reminded those to whom he wrote that we all should aspire to godly contentment. Yet change was just over his horizon. His first letter of 2011 greeted me thusly:

"Happy New Year! How are you and Deanna doing? What challenges have you two set up for the year?

For me, there have been some profound changes. The first was that I lost my trustee job. One of the guys went off about his tray. He had saved up some feces in bottles and some urine. He slung it all up and down the tier. Awful rank stuff! He got it on the juice cover too. The officers called the watch commander to address the problems. He didn't, but instead began cleaning up the mess. The guys were really abusing him because he was the ranking officer. Yet he could not order the officers under him to clean up the mess. They had him irate; I'd never seen him that mad. He had no one to vent on until he remembered me. He came to my door to tell me to clean up the mess or I was fired. He sounded like Donald Trump as a drill sergeant.

Cleaning up the mess was not addressing the problems. More feces were flung, and then several of the guys got in on the act. The tier was trashed, and a fire was set. If this had been anywhere else, they would have called it rioting.

So, of course not; I am not coming out of my cell! The tier is crazy, going off, and I need to get out of the way and stay out of the way.

The w.c. (watch commander) sees things are really bad news, but he still wants to push me out there. I refuse. He now recognizes that things are getting out of hand. He calls for a K-9 with a block gun, a warden and a dozen officers to back him up.

The w.c. is losing his head; he keeps telling me to clean up the tier. I tell him I'm not refusing to work, but I am refusing to get my head busted. It's happened a dozen times where the tier has gone off, he comes to address the problem and largely cleans up the mess. When feelings calm down, I come out to clean up the rest.

But this time the w.c. wanted to put me out there before the fire was out. I refused, and he argued that my refusal to come out was refusal to work and therefore grounds for my termination. He just wanted to use me as a vent, an outlet for his anger. I hated to lose the job, but I don't regret my decision.

I have tried to get the job back; but as luck would have it, the w.c., at 32, became the captain here at (my unit). He still refuses to let me out and says that he will consider me in 90 days. He has to feel like he is the man and thump his chest. That's cool to me; he can do his thing, because I know in 90 days he will be back trying to get me to work. There are too few people that can actually attain the trustee position, so he doesn't have a pool to draw upon. He'll be back, and I'm willing to bet before the 90 days are up." (1-21-11).

Joe proved to be something of a prophet when he wrote again in May:

"April had some good spots. I got my trustee job back. The w.c. at (my previous unit) was the one that fired me. He became the captain here at (my present unit). Despite my best efforts, I was not able to convince him to let me back out. Then I came to find out that he didn't have the authority to fire me for the way things went down in December. The best he could do was give me a 90-day suspension. And even then he was reluctant. I had not had a urine test in years, but suddenly, the urine man was at my door. If the captain can find me to have hot urine, then he could fire me. I was clean. Then I had a 'random' shakedown. If the captain can find my cell to have contraband, then he can fire me. My cell also was clean. And then finally, he let me back out.

I so love the movement again. The cleaning is largely the same, so no trouble there. The best part is that I don't have to deal with BSOC – the cameras – again. They hassled me to no end at (my previous unit), but I fear I won't have it much longer. I figure because I'm short time, that they will come to take the job before too much longer." (5-25-11).

Undoubtedly, Joe was beginning to realize that his time might be running out, for he ended this letter with the following comments:

Bishop____ came to visit us for Lent in April. I really like talking to him. He told me of grassroot

efforts to abolish the death penalty here in
____. I told him I was starved for that kind of
information, because I had so little access to it. I
asked him to send me the names and addresses of
various politicians and organizations that I could
write to about it. I never heard back from him.
Now I am resorting to asking everyone I can to
send me this information so I can begin a serious
writing campaign.

May turned out to be a horrible month. We have
had two executions – Billy Paul Justins on May
10th and Rob Roy White on May 17th. Another
man was supposed to die yesterday, but thankfully
he was given a stay. Not sure if it is a permanent
one yet. Three of us have lost our appeals so we
are next in line.

Dave, I desperately need your and Deanna's voice
before Governor ____. To ask him for (and receive)
clemency, would be to spare me the death penalty;
and then I would receive a life-without-parole
sentence.

I do hate this place, but I would gladly withstand
all the rigors this place has to offer if I could
live out my life. But I need a consolidated voice
of people out there to help me. Any and every
person that might be willing to help would be
wonderfully welcome.

I need to close here. There are so many people I want to ask to help me, so much to write, so much to ask, so much to still live for. Please help me...

P.S. A good note – Happy Birthday to you, Deanna!" (5-21-11).

CHAPTER 3

Joe, the Scholar

A scholar is defined as a learned person; one having much knowledge. Obviously then, one who thirsts for knowledge would be one whose scholarship increases with access to and use of learning tools.

Joe finished high school in the middle 1990s. Whether or not he intended to attend college, I don't know; but what I learned about him through our years of writing made me confident that he would have been a successful college student. His interests and passions were many and varied, and he developed and maintained a strenuous regimen during his years of incarceration. I was amazed at his accomplishments given the limitations of a non-academic environment.

What a contrast his self-discipline was to the routines of most of his fellow-inmates. While he and the others on death-row had only minimal contact, many of them managed to communicate and build a body of knowledge, albeit cursory, about one another. In Joe's infrequent comments about some of his colleagues, he usually spoke disparagingly and with considerable disappointment. Obviously their chosen lifestyles in confinement were far different from his.

After we had exchanged letters for about six months, I was impressed by his wide range of interests. I wrote:

> "I appreciate your inquisitiveness; you are interested in so many things. How I hope that you will receive release from your conviction and sentence so that you can find a free pursuit of a life's goal!" (4-4-00).

Joe replied:

> "You wrote that I have many things that I'm interested in. Only if you knew, Dave. There are hundreds of things that I'd love to know and do. I've always wanted to be a writer. It's the oldest dream I've had and it's never left. I want to be a truck driver for many reasons: to travel the country seeing new sights and people; to do something that is vital to this country; to do something that is decent and worthwhile; and to be around diesels. Metallurgy would be another field of interest. One time when I was little, I got a desire to be a marine biologist, but I'm afraid of sharks. Being a journalist has tickled my fancy a time or two. Oh yes, I read a book recently by a British author named James Herriott. He had me wanting to be a veterinarian. And, of course, I would like some form of military career. That dream is almost as old as the writing one." (4-11-00)

Interestingly, Joe closed this early letter with these words: "Dave, with all sincerity, if they were to let me go today I would be afraid to so much as get a traffic ticket. Maybe I've learned what society has been trying to get across all along." Twelve years later, when I wrote to the state governor in Joe's behalf, I remembered this comment as I argued that Joe would be a low-risk recidivist.

Joe read widely though he was limited by the availability of good, challenging books. Seldom did I receive a letter in which one or more books were not mentioned; and most of these he had read or hoped to read. Consider these examples from his letters:

> "Have you been following the debates among academics on Intelligent Design? Some of the technical stuff is quite mind-numbing. In one book by Michael Behe, he warns that the reader might want to get an introductory book in bio-chemistry." (1-2-00).

> "We've been able to order a second set of books from the library. My choices this time were <u>War and Peace</u> by Leo Tolstoy and the second volume of Churchill's rendering of World War II.... This week I ordered <u>Paranormal Phenomena</u>. The second was <u>Les Miserables</u> by Victor Hugo. The third was <u>Encyclopedia of Dreams</u>." (1-18-01).

> "Have you read any Dan Brown books? I read his <u>Angels and Demons</u> and really enjoyed it. I've been waiting on <u>The Divinci Code</u> to come out in paperback... Have you read any of Jean Auel's books? I finished the fifth volume of her 'Earth's

Children' series, <u>The Shelter of Stone</u>. I've enjoyed them all." (3-13-05).

"For my birthday I got <u>SAT Math Mania</u>. I am not taking the test, but I needed to rework and learn new math problems that I learned in school and forgot and some that I never did... I was looking to get the <u>SAT Verbal Velocity</u> because I really want to work on my vocabulary... I'm especially interested in the verbal because I have been doing a lot of writing lately... I write a short story every month." (1-5-07).

Death-row inmates ordinarily spend the great majority of their time in their cells. Typically one hour per day is given for outside activities – recreation, exercise and such. After being locked up for several years, Joe landed a trusty's job. This afforded him opportunity to work outside the cell on his tier in general cleaning activities.

My point here is that while most of his contemporaries were content to vegetate – doing little or nothing – Joe had a strict regimen that compelled him to set and meet monthly and annual goals. Much of this involved reading, writing, improving vocabulary and keeping records of his success/progress.

In 2008, Joe wrote:

"I recently came across another article on the scientist (Hermann Elbinghaus). It talked of his studies in learning in a structured method with spacing effect and testing to discover one's moment of forgetfulness. This inspired me to conduct my own experiment on my memory. I have committed myself to learning the Periodic Table. Once done, I plan to test myself in two months' time to determine how much I've retained." (5-29-08).

In 2009, Joe resolved to learn a new word each week. He explained it this way:

> "I have at least one resolution for 2009: I am going to learn a new word each Sunday. During that week I will practice it over and over again in my letters. In the process I can probably teach someone else a new word too." (12-28-08).

> "With 52 weeks in the year I can go through the alphabet twice. Week one was 'atavism,' and week four is 'doldrums.' I am writing out the definitions to help me learn them." (1-30-09).

> "My vocabulary words have been 'obtuse,' 'plenary,' quotidian,' 'Roche limit'" (6-8-09).

In 2001, after learning of our mutual interests in military affairs, I was able to have the *Air Force Magazine* mailed to Joe monthly. He wrote: "It gets some circulation here. Two pilots, one a Viet Nam vet, particularly like them. There is another VN vet who was a Seabee, who reads them too." (8-08-01).

Later in that same letter, Joe wrote:

> "There's something I want to ask you. When you were teaching did you have a reading list you either had your students read or recommended?

What I'm doing now is trying to read some of the classics. They are now letting books of no specific genre come in though they are still enforcing the soft book policy.* I gave Mama several to get for me, but I'm looking for what James V. Schall, a Jesuit, calls liberal education books. Liberal in the generous and bountiful sense, I think. Maybe open-minded, too.

One that Schall recommended, and I put on my list to Mama, was Plato's *The Republic.* I wrote in search of the book that Schall wrote that told of this liberal education that he recommended. That will help in that sense. But I wanted to know what you recommend.

Some others that I wrote Mama about are (1) James Joyce's *Ulysses*; (2) Johann Wolfgang Von Goethe's *Faust* and *Mephistopheles;* (3) Thomas Mann's *Dr. Faustus*; (4) Aristotle's *Organon;* (5) Niccolo Machiavelli's *The Prince;* and (6) Sun Tzu's *The Art of War*...

I will tell you a problem that I've encountered in my readings. I've come across an acute bout of eclecticism. At points I believe that it may be the cause of depression that I go through. I've asked myself, what am I learning or have I learned in my reading? Has it given me any insight about life or who I am? I don't know the answer to any

---

*   Joe's prison allowed no hard-bound books.

of those questions. I wonder: are my thoughts my own – can I think of anything that's sapient? Do I have the right to be wise or author some form of wisdom?

Here's my conundrum: I want to be wise but don't want the pride that goes with it. I want to be known to be wise but fear being shown that I know nothing of importance. I want to be able to express myself and someone understand me. Have I made sense to you?"

Joe was making good sense to me. While he was not yet a polished writer, his enthusiasm and resolve were exceptional. One of his short stories is at Appendix A.

CHAPTER 4

Joe, the Saint

Early on in my correspondence with Joe, I became committed to the hope of encouraging him in as many ways as possible. Because I am a God-fearer (fearer=respecter) and a disciple of His Son, Jesus, I wanted Joe to know about God, the Creator-Sustainer and Jesus, the Savior-Redeemer. Consequently, I often took easy opportunities to address spiritual concerns. He spoke often of his views of capital punishment and what it meant to him to be on death row. Putting myself in his place, I thought it important to speak of Christ's victory over physical death and the hope that Christians have in a spiritual, and later, a bodily resurrection.

In keeping with this chapter title, I must explain why I feel that Joe is a saint. The apostle Paul speaks often of saints in his New Testament letters. He uses the Greek term *hagios* (literally "holy one") or plural, *hagioi* ("holy ones") to designate simply believers or church members, who are believers and set apart for service to God. This distinction differs from the traditions of certain groups' practice of canonization, the declaration of a person (usually deceased) to be a saint and to be placed in the official list of saints. Ordinarily, in such traditions, official canonization follows beatification, a formal declaration, by the church's head, that a dead person is among the blessed in heaven and deserves religious honor. Such saints are called Saint ____, the masculine title, or Sainte ____, the feminine title, abbreviated respectively St. and Ste.

What do God's 'holy ones' say and do? What do they believe and profess? What is their outlook on life – and death? Perhaps some answers to these and other questions may be seen in the comments that Joe made through the years. In our first year as pen-pals, he wrote:

> "Now I myself claim to be a Christian. On October 18, 1995 I accepted the Lord into my life. Little did I know what I was doing then, but now I have learned a lot and have a long way to go. I have been able to see the difference He has made in my life. The irony is finding life in God by going to death row. All in all it is much better this route than to never find Life in God.
>
> I don't know what your denomination is, but that is irrelevant as long as we can agree on the Apostle's Creed. My denomination would be 'non-denominational.' I don't adhere to any one though I have considered the Society of Jesus, which – if you've never heard of – is Catholic. My favorite saint is Saint Ignatius who founded the Society. He lived from 1491-1556" (10-19-99).
>
> "Before God was part of my life I had an atheistic/epicureanism mentality. I didn't know then what I know now, or I would of known that it was all meaningless. Have you ever read 'A Shattered

29

Visage – the True Face of Atheism' by Ravi Zacharias? It's a good book; I recommend it if you haven't" (11-3-99).

"A new year, decade, century, and millennium! Let's hope and pray that something good becomes of the future. We know Jesus' second coming is in the future, so we don't have to worry about that" (1-2-00).

"You told me to be like Paul once who was unjustly imprisoned. I cannot do so. Paul was so much more righteous than I. We would be a bad comparison. I will concur that I feel that things I claim to be innocent of the present charge, I am no less guilty for my others. James 2:10 teaches that if we commit one sin, we have committed them all. In that light I am guilty.

When we commit a sin, we must accept the subsequent consequences. Sin begets more sin, if we don't take advantage of the wonderful act of repentance. I know this truth and yet I still fail. It has made me ponder the reason we are so attracted toward sin in the first place." (1-19-00).

Because righteousness is not always a concept easily grasped, I wanted to add my thoughts to Joe's understanding. Also, I wanted to affirm his thoughts on sin's attractiveness. Here is part of my response in a letter dated January 25, 2000:

"Returning to my suggestion of your emulation of Paul who was unjustly imprisoned, you replied 'Paul was much more righteous than I.' That is incorrect, Joe! <u>All believers</u> get their righteousness from God's Son, and He doesn't give it in degrees. It is all the same! Righteousness means to be in right relationship with God the Father. When we confess and repent of our sins, we instantly are <u>made right</u> with God. This is because of Jesus' work on the cross. He died for our sins – <u>all of them</u>. We must repent of all of our sins and continue to do so, because we do not become sinless until we reach heaven.

You wonder why we are so attracted to sin? First, I believe that Satan makes it very appealing to us (read Genesis 3 of Eve's encounter with the serpent – especially verse 6). Then read Romans – chapters 5 through 8 for Paul's insight into sin. Read 2 Corinthians 5:21 for his statement on righteousness." (1-25-00).

In early 2001, Joe had just completed the reading of the epic, *Quo Vadis*. He was so moved by its message, he felt that he needed to immediately put pen to paper:

"I write to you moments after finishing a most enrapturing, thrilling, informative, and exciting novel. One that I recommend that you at once purchase. If you have already read it, then I feel you will have some idea as to how I feel. You may have even more fitting adjectives to describe it.

The novel in question is *Quo Vadis*. It was written by Henryk Sienkiewicz. It's long at some 579 pages but well worth the time to read. I wonder if anyone cannot be moved to a higher dedication or awareness of God. I wonder if that person who is not moved by the reading of this book is beyond rescue. We know that all can be saved by Jesus; it's the magnitude of the total absorption that the book gets you. That's why I use the description 'beyond rescue.'" (2-11-01).

On March the 22nd I got baptized. I was also confirmed into the Catholic Church and took part in communion. That was a pretty cool day.

The head Bishop... performed the rites. It was kind of strange going through the procedures because they were so formal and serious. I was given a baptismal stole once the ceremony was over. It was really long, white and had a blue cross on it. I wore it for a few seconds only because I am not allowed to have it in my possession.

I also got a godfather in the process. No, not one like Marlon Brando! He's a spiritual adviser not a criminal adviser. His name is Gerald Danforth; he and a Father McVicker come to visit us each month.

Some people won't understand, but I'm sure you will. Since the baptism I have felt really good – mentally and physically! I have been in a mental lethargy for a long time, but I feel good now. It's like good things are on the horizon and most everything else doesn't matter.

I've been really lazy for some time now. I walk as much as I can and have started a small, beginning workout. I blame it on God! I truly believe that the baptism was the advent of experiencing God like I have not done since I have become a Christian!!

I still can't find the proper words to express how I feel. It's as if I have been taking 'energy' pills. That's not a good analogy; it's like I've caught a second wind advancing to God." (4-2-02).

Because these experiences seemed to have such an impact on Joe, I felt it appropriate to respond in a way to try to keep this topic open for future discussions:

"I was interested in reading about your confirmation into the Roman Catholic Church. To the Church and to you, what do baptism and communion mean? Those are the two ordinances in my church, and I'm interested in knowing how they compare – in mode and meaning.

I'm pleased to read that you have felt something of a transformation in your life. You say that you can't find proper words to express your feelings? As time goes on perhaps you'll be able to express those feelings better. I'd be interested in hearing those thoughts." (5-15-02).

One week later, in his next letter, Joe brought up the topics of his recent baptism and participation in communion:

> "The baptism went like this: prayers were said over the water, then it wasn't a complete submersion, just a small bottle poured over the head. The bishop said, as he did so, 'I baptize you in the name of the Father, the Son, and the Holy Spirit.'
>
> That would be the only difference in mode – not complete submersion in water. The meaning should be the same for both of us: symbolic burial and resurrection from the grave as Jesus was, to come to a new life clean.
>
> For communion we partook of bread and juice. I've heard two interpretations of this: one being symbolic of the flesh and blood of Jesus; the other being literal. The Catholic church believes that it is literal. I don't have a problem with either interpretation because both are being done in remembrance of Jesus and should be taken seriously.
>
> I take communion with both Catholics and Episcopalians. The bishop may not approve but again it's communion with Jesus. Some things should transcend the denomination; such as the creed bringing the faith in oneness. Communion, to me, should be no different.

The mode is just that the body of Christ comes in a snap-shut case, and there's a neat goblet to drink from." (5-22-02).

Joe had a keen interest in games and puzzles. Early in our correspondence, he wondered if we might try playing chess through the mail. Later he asked if I'd ever played Scrabble. Once, I sent him a list of 15 well-known sayings that had been rewritten - camouflaged with numerous less well-known words. For example, what is this well-known saying: 'As with the sire, so it is with the scion'? 'Like father, like son.' Joe was able to correctly answer 13 of the 15.

Because of our mutual interest in the Bible, he often asked questions about certain passages and commented on other passages. To stimulate his questioning mind, and to provide an opportunity to fill any down-time he might have, I challenged him to a bit of biblical research. In my letter of February 1, 2003, I wrote:

> "I asked if you'd like to study and discuss some passages in the Bible, and you concurred. Why don't we begin with the following passages:
>
> 1. 2 Samuel 11 and 12
> 2. Psalms 32 and 51

And the following questions:

> 1. Who was David?
> 2. What was his relationship with God?
> 3. What sins did he commit?

4. What were some of the results of these sins? (see 2 Samuel 13-18)

5. How are Psalms 32 and 51 related to this part of David's story?

6. How are these passages related to you and the other inmates at ____?"

Joe's responses came two months later:

"I have reviewed the passages in the Bible you referred to and here are the answers to the Questions:

(1) Who was David? David was the second king of Israel anointed by Samuel, Saul being the first king.

(2) What was his relationship with God? At first, David had an intimate relationship with God that fell apart with David's adultery with Bathsheba, his murder of Uriah, Bathsheba's husband, and the treachery involved in it all.

(3) What sins did he commit? Answer above; in short, adultery, murder and deception.

(4) What were some of the results of these sins? This made me think of the quote that 'the sins of the father are visited upon the sons.' The problem was that I could not find where that verse is. I asked a friend where it might be located and he thought it was in Deuteronomy but couldn't give

me any more specifics. I say this because the first result of David's sins was the death of the boy Bathsheba gave him. I found six other sins that could be argued as a result of David's. The domino effect seems to have occurred.

(5) How are Psalms 32 and 51 related to this part of David's story? The Psalms are David's confessions and where he asks God to forgive his sins. What's noteworthy here is that though David confessed his sins, asked God's forgiveness, and it was granted, the domino effect of sin seems not to have stopped. Why? Too many sins. It was as if David picked up a sin then realized what it was and repented. Instead of trying to avoid all sin, he picked up another (that of not reconciling with Absalom) and put it in his pocket. These chapters conveyed an example of 'perpetual sin,' if there is such a concept. This goes directly into the next question:

(6) How are these passages related to you and the other inmates at ___? Sinning for the sake of sinning as if it is the last chance at autonomy – 'I' can do this because 'I' want to. I don't know if the last sentence answers the question or what I have in my head that I can't convey. Perpetual sin? Sin got us here, sin keeps us here, sin has control over us. How to avoid this – 'perpetual repentance' I suppose.

How did I do? My last answer feels lacking and I don't know what to add. It's like the saying: 'it's on the tip of my tongue, but it just won't come out.'" (4-6-03).

I was astonished at the breadth of insight that Joe revealed in these answers to the questions that I had sent, and I was pleased with the way he related the thoughts to himself and his fellow inmates. I wondered if he had read of the apostle Paul's personal struggle with sin as he wrote in his letter to the church in Rome: "I do not understand what I do. For what I want to do, I do not do, but what I hate I do... What a wretched man I am! Who will rescue me from this body of death? Thanks be to God – through Jesus Christ our Lord! *(Romans 7:15,24-25)*.

Joe's letter of May 29, 2008 took us in a different direction and brought in the thoughts of another of his pen-pals:

"I have kept my daily reading of the Bible going. I have made it all the way through Psalms, which took me a month to complete. I've been through Proverbs and liked it a lot. Several of them reminded me of my dad, the one that died in '98; a wise man was lost. I'm in Ecclesiastes at the moment.

Now I'll segue into a Jehovah's Witness I write to. She and I have been discussing soul-sleep. She favors it; I do not. I wrote an essay years ago stating my view. One of my defenses was Luke 23:43. I argued that Jesus telling the thief that he would be in Paradise with Him that day as an example of souls' not sleeping because the thief would have to be awake and aware to realize Jesus' promise. One of her responses was rather provocative. Let me write out the verse as it is in my Bible and how she says it should be.

'Assuredly, I say to you, today you will be with me in Paradise.' Her rendition: 'Assuredly, I say to you today, you will be with me in Paradise.' Do you see how the placement of the comma drastically changes the intent of Jesus' words?

Susan, the woman's name I write to, says that it is the fault of biased translators that they would place the comma in the wrong place.

I would like your help with an appropriate response. She makes a logical argument. If simple placement is involved, then I need to know which is correct. How do I convince her that the Bible has the correct placement and do so with a reasoned logical response?"

In my responses to Joe's questions, I tried to make four points:

"Joe, I had to do some investigative research regarding your comments/questions on Luke 23:43. Interestingly, my CBS (Community Bible Study) class at the Penitentiary of New Mexico was finishing up our study of *Luke's* Gospel, so I took your letter with me as we studied *Luke 23*. It was a good opportunity to make a point about a faulty translation. I also discussed the verse with my pastor, and he showed me the verse in Greek along with the commentary provided. Here are my summary findings:

1. Original texts of the Old Testament in Hebrew and Aramaic and the New Testament in Greek and Aramaic had <u>no punctuation</u>. Punctuation marks were added to the manuscripts centuries later by translators/interpreters.

2. Every reputable translation into English punctuates verse 23 so that it is understood to read 'today you will be with Me in Paradise." Clearly the New World translation used by your Jehovah's Witness pen-pal is <u>not what the writer intended</u>.

3. *Luke 23:43* is one of the many glimpses we have of heaven from God's written Word. Read *Luke 16:19-31*. What does this glimpse of heaven, given by Jesus, suggest to you about 'soul-sleep' vis-à-vis immediately going to heaven or hell?

4. My paternal grandparents were Jehovah's Witnesses. My grandfather taught from the New World translation, and I heard him speak often of 'soul-sleep.' In my opinion, the Bible, correctly translated, does not teach such a doctrine." (7-5-08).

The change came abruptly! On death row, execution is always a prospect, but somehow expectation gets pushed to the recesses of one's mind. This is especially true when one has gone through a lengthy process of appeals. Joe had been incarcerated for more than a dozen years when he wrote in mid-2011:

"Hello, my friend. I hope you and Deanna are well and taking care. I write with a heavy heart. I have lost my latest appeal and am terrified beyond belief. I had so much of my hopes and dreams invested in this appeal. It's devastating to have lost. The first day I learned of the bad news I was in straight panic mode. I've calmed down a little as I have been able to access the situation, talk to my attorney, and begin a strategy on how to move forward.

John, the attorney, describes the remaining legal avenues as this: A petition for rehearing has to filed in two weeks – that makes the due date of June 2. He expects the court to dismiss that within 30 days. From there the appeal –writ of certiorari – to the U.S. Supreme Court has to be filed within 90 days. The state will file their brief in October or November. The court could kick the appeal out, and the A.G. (attorney general) would ask for a date of execution 30 days from there. Late January it should all be over with.

The more I recite the last months of my life, the more it twists my stomach. I am so scared, Dave. I am in a desperate state and need all the help I can get. Will you be a voice of clemency before the Governor? I need as many voices as possible. I need more people asking to spare me than clamoring to kill me!

Right now I am in a disorganized state because I have no single vehicle to bring people together. I badly need that and am in search of that. I want to put everyone on the same page." (5-25-11).

This news was devastating to Deanna and me as well. We were hoping that our criminal justice system would somehow get it right: exonerate an innocent man and find the truly guilty person. I was concerned, also, that Satan would use these events to cause Joe to question his status with God. Accordingly, I quickly wrote back to Joe:

"Thank you for sharing your bad news with Deanna and me. We are praying for God's will, as we've been doing for the past 12 years; and we know He will bring you exoneration or clemency, or He will call you home, because you are His adopted son. Whatever His will may be, you will be victorious because you belong to Him!

I trust that you recognize what I have said above is what I have talked to you about in most of my correspondence with you these past 12 years. If you believe what I say, you have no reason to be in panic mode. If you don't understand what I have said, I certainly have misunderstood what you have written to me over these years." (6-7-11).

Only six weeks passed until I heard from Joe again, yet he apologized for the delay. Though he obviously was climbing out of the throes of depression, his spiritual life had taken a hit.

"I apologize for not getting your letter written last month. I was out of it. I lost my motivation, I felt defeated, I was tired. I missed a lot of letters last month; you weren't the only one. In fact, most of the month's letters were poorly done or not done at all. Two days I actually did not write a letter at all. That was the first time 4 ½ years that I had failed to do that. Letters weren't the only thing that suffered. I missed six yard calls, and I had resolved not to miss any. My workout regimen disappeared; I literally felt devastated.

But then comes July with a chance to get back on the wagon, recommit, fight on. My letters are flying out the door, and they have substance and coherence. I do admit there are four letters that did not get completed on their assigned days. I'm still working to get them done. But four is so much less than 20. The point is to keep at it no matter what.

Your letter was the usual thought-provoking way. It demanded that I re-evaluate just what it is that I believe. If I believe that I am a saved man and heaven is my final destination, some of that fear should be mitigated. Intellectually, I agree with that. But I think I'm emotionally immature as a Christian. My whole approach to Christianity has been logical and methodical. I haven't explored the depths of my emotional attachment to the faith, or the lack thereof.

When you know there is a part of you that you haven't explored, you know there is a part of you that you haven't abandoned to God. And therein lies the consuming fear. I believe in God. I believe that Jesus Christ died on the cross to save us all. But... but I know I ain't right before God. I fear that I can't be, that there is a part of me that holds me back. And how do I face death knowing that?

How do I abandon that part, mature on that level, when I have built a defense mechanism to do the opposite of that? I know that every time I pleaded in my head that 'I ain't ready,' there was a part of me that was comforted with that. 'I ain't ready:' is that acknowledgment of something wrong? Is it recognition of a problem? Not a quick fix!" (7-21-11).

Because Joe had raised several questions in the letter just quoted and was obviously struggling with his faith as his time apparently was running out, I felt that I should respond right away. While I did not want to give him a false hope, I wanted to assure him that God's love and grace would see him through any eventuality. My response will end this chapter, but more will be said at the book's conclusion.

"As I review your last letter (7-21-11), I'm grateful for your comment, 'Your letter was the usual thought-provoking way.' As a former professor and as a current Bible teacher (both inside and outside a prison), I feel a responsibility to provoke others (in the best sense of that term). In that regard, I want to comment on a couple of your observations:

1. 'My whole approach to Christianity has been logical and methodical.' This is natural and okay <u>as far as it goes</u>. The human brain by weight compared to our body weight is much greater than any others of God's creatures. So, we have the great ability to reason; but too many of us put <u>all</u> our eggs in the basket of rationality and science. God demands faith (belief and trust in Him, Who can be known but not seen). 'Faith is being sure of what we hope for and certain of what we do not see... And without faith it is impossible to please God, because anyone who comes to Him must believe that He exists and that he rewards those who earnestly seek Him' *(Hebrews 11:1,6)*.

2. 'But... but I know I ain't right before God. I fear that I can't be, that there is a part of me that holds me back. And how do I face death knowing that?' Right means righteousness (having a right relationship with God). Righteousness begins with faith: 'Abram (Abraham) believed the Lord, and He (the Lord) credited it to him as righteousness' *(Genesis 15:6)*. The apostle Paul quoted this verse in his letter to the Romans: 'What does the Scripture say? Abraham believed God, and it was credited to him as righteousness.' *(Romans 4:3)*. Earlier in the letter, Paul had said this: 'For in the gospel a righteousness from God is revealed, a righteousness that is by faith from first to last, just as it is written: The righteous will live by faith.' *(Habakkuk 2:4; Romans 1:17)*. So, Joe, one becomes right with

God through faith in Jesus Christ. Paul put it this way in his second letter to the Corinthians: 'God made Him (Jesus) who had no sin to be sin for us, so that in Him we might become the righteousness of God' *(2 Corinthians 5:21)*. If you belong to Christ, as you say you do, you are ready for death!!!' (8-29-11).

CHAPTER 5

Joe, the Anti-Death Penalty Advocate

Please be prepared to find in this chapter our most gut-wrenching exchanges. If you have had no personal struggles with the issues surrounding the pros and cons of capital punishment and related topics, you may find our views quite challenging.

The first murder recorded in the Bible was Cain's slaying of Abel. It happened after the "fall" of humankind into sinful disobedience of God's moral pronouncement: "You are free to eat from any tree in the garden, but you must not eat from the tree of the knowledge of good and evil, for when you eat of it you will surely die" (*Genesis 2:16-17*). If you don't know this story, Adam and Eve ate the fruit of that tree (*Genesis 3:1-19*) and, later, they died as God had promised (*Genesis 5:5*).

The brief story of Cain and Abel is given in *Genesis 4:1-16*. After Cain killed Abel, he was punished – banished from the Garden of Eden out of God's presence. Before the banishment, however, we find this dialogue between the Lord God and Cain: "Then the Lord said to Cain, 'Where is your brother Abel? 'I don't know,' he replied, 'Am I my brother's keeper?'" This exchange brings us the first question of moral responsibility for another human; how are we to answer that question? And similarly, how are we to answer today this question: "What are we to do with a person who murders another person?"

From the outset of our exchanging of letters, I sought to ascertain whether or not Joe had in fact taken the life of the woman he was convicted of murdering. In his third letter, Joe wrote:

> "Now the tough question; tough because I feel you are – as the legal terminology goes – laying the proper predicate. 'Why are you appealing your conviction and sentence?' (This was my question to Joe). What do you want – the legal answer or the philosophical? If I believe in God as much as I say I do, why appeal? Why not let the chips fall as they may? I don't think that it is limited to just trying to regain physical freedom. Though the answer hasn't been fully given to me, the legal and philosophical aspects may coincide.
>
> I want to appeal because I don't feel my trial was fair. I have instances of inadmissible testimony, perjured testimony, discovery violations and prosecutorial misconduct. Let me stop; my case should be in a Southern Reporter Second Edition by now. Have you read it? I don't know the cite, but I believe it should be there. My direct appeal was... remanded back for a Batson hearing. I assume you're familiar with this, if not I'll explain

it in a subsequent letter... The appeal of that hearing will be filed later this month.

The whole issue of the death penalty in this country is that it is a farce. It's inconsistent, racial, and arbitrary. I wish to fight against that; to argue for those rights that were proscribed to me and have those applicable laws that affect me enforced as they were designed for.

The philosophical aspect – I don't feel that society at large can support the death penalty as proscribed by God as has been the argument in the past. Jesus never preached enforcement of the death penalty even when faced with the situation that warranted it. Society can't look to the O.T. (Old Testament) for support because it's not supportive of the present practice.

I'm here because allegedly I committed a murder and sexual assault upon a woman. You wrote that you were not being nosy or trying to pry – in reference to fully understanding why I am here; that you knew Someone who can help me eternally. What does that mean? You know I am a Christian, that heaven is my destination, but you still wish to know these things because you know Someone. The logic has eschewed me. So please help me understand your motives for these inquiries.

And finally, I'm appealing my conviction because life is beautiful. I want to enjoy it. Enjoy it, but not in this manner. I abhor the company here and its various rigors.

Here's a question for you. Why do you jump out of the way of a speeding train?" (11-3-99).

Joe's concerns were reasonable, but I needed to understand his motives: did he misunderstand what I had said or was he wondering why I said what I did? To continue our dialogue and clarify what and why, I responded:

"... what I have said about Christianity is a bridge to comment on your situation/case. I apologize if I have seemed vague with my questions to you. I will be more succinct.

I asked why you are appealing your case. Legal and/or philosophical answers may be important now, but in eternity they are quite unimportant! You said, 'I'm here because allegedly I committed a murder and sexual assault upon a woman.' The term allege means 'assertion without proof.' Since most criminals do not come forward and confess their crime(s), society must grapple with the determination of guilt. Part of our society (those connected with your trial) have heard the evidence presented and determined that you are guilty. If your appeal is granted, another part of society will grapple with your case again.

I assume that there was (is) a dead woman who did not take her own life and who was sexually assaulted. I very desperately want you to write in your next letter, 'Dave, I did not commit those crimes!' if that is the truth.

On the other hand, if you did, in fact, commit those crimes, you know it and God knows it. That makes you a murderer and, if you pleaded innocent, that makes you also a liar. If you cannot write to me, 'Dave, I did not commit those crimes! You must confess it to God, and you must ask God if you should confess it to someone else (such as the court, the victim's family, etc.). These crimes are forgivable, and one's eternal salvation rests on contrition, confession, repentance and forgiveness. If you are guilty and if you have a Bible, I recommend that you read the following passages: *2 Samuel 11:1-12, Psalms 32 and 51, Hebrews* 4:12-13 and *Revelation 20:12-13*. These passages clearly show God's provisions and requirements regarding our sins.

To summarize then, here is what I asked you in my first letter: 'If we continue to correspond, you can count on me to be truthful and candid with you; in turn, I expect the same from you. When you write again, please explain why you are on death row.' In my second letter, I wrote: 'By the way, it is imperative that I understand fully why you are on death row... it is because I know Someone who can help you eternally.'

You say that you are a Christian and that heaven is your destination; I say praise the Lord and I rejoice with you! But I warn you, unless you are innocent of these crimes, I urge you to reconsider what God demands of us regarding confession and repentance. If you are innocent which means you were falsely accused and convicted, I urge your continuation of your appeal. You need to be exonerated, and the real murderer needs to be apprehended. Don't you agree that society has a right to know that s(he) won't kill someone else?

As I close, I'll take a stab at answering your last question, 'why do you jump out of the way of a speeding train?' My answer, which is probably the same as yours, is 'to keep from getting hit (or killed) by the train.' The question, I feel, is irrelevant to your case. What is more relevant to your case is this question, 'why would I (or you) be walking on or driving across a train track where we should know that speeding trains often travel?'" (11-16-99).

Looking back at these letters, I feel that Joe and I were doing little more than sparring (feeling one another out). Heavier blows were soon to come; Joe's next letter came quickly:

"You asked me to write 'Dave, I did not commit those crimes!' I've been saying that from day one and no one has believed me, save for my family. If I were to say that, what would it mean to you? Would you have instant belief in me or would you still grapple with the answer you think is true?

Would the latter grappling situation be due to your subjective influences from your time with society or criminal institutions? Or would you view my answer objectively and take me at my word?

I say, Dave, I did not commit those crimes. It seems utterly redundant, but if it will satisfy your objective or subjective needs, I'll comply.

I asked the question 'Why would you jump out of the way of a speeding train?' You said it was irrelevant to my case. I concur, but the question was in regards to your question, 'Why are you appealing your case?' To me both questions had self-evident answers." (11-28-99).

How grateful I was to hear Joe say that he didn't commit those crimes. This admission cleared away the first of several hurdles that we were to encounter, so that we could move on to some other issues. Nevertheless, I had to acknowledge his confession, so I wrote the following month:

"Joe, I am very relieved to hear you say that you did not murder and sexually assault that woman! Since you have told me this, I believe you! Let me try to explain my concern. If you have any conversations with any of your fellow death-row inmates, have you any notion of how many of the total are guilty of the crime(s) and are appealing their cases because of some technicality of the law (e.g., their rights were violated, they were not read their Miranda rights, evidence of guilt had to be thrown out, etc.)? Until you told me, how did I know why you were appealing your conviction?

In my mind, there is a great difference in appealing because of <u>innocence</u> and appealing because of <u>violation of a technicality in man's imperfect judicial system</u>. In eternity, it matters <u>little</u> if one's rights in court are violated; whether one commits a crime matters <u>greatly</u> – it can be the difference between heaven and hell! I trust you understand fully the import of what I have said.

You are an innocent man who has been convicted of a heinous crime. I hope that your appeal will be successful, and that the real criminal will be apprehended. If he is, what do you think he deserves?

All of this is the reason I agreed to correspond with you. I want the <u>truth</u> about your situation, for only in the truth is there the opportunity for salvation. I trust that I have the truth in regard to your innocence. Think of yourself as a Paul, who was imprisoned unjustly. Read of his joy – while in prison – in his letter to the Philippians. Can you claim some of that kind of joy while you wait to see what God has in store for you? It is a lot to ask of a youngster like you, but with God's power, all things are possible!" (12-16-99).

After these exchanges, perhaps it could be concluded that Joe and I had reached an uneasy truce: he vowed his innocence, and I vowed to accept his avowal. Interestingly, the topic of death was soon broached again – from a different viewpoint. In early 2000, Joe wrote his views of abortion:

"Recently I've pondered the nefarious spectacle of abortion. The slogan goes 'a woman's right to choose – her right to choose.'

When a woman exclaims this narcissism does the question arise 'where does this right originate?' Surely it doesn't, or if so I missed the reigning logic. Say that the woman's answer to this right's origin comes from God. She at some point would have to say that God condones the murder of babies. But doesn't that fall apart in the face of the sixth commandment? Logically, she couldn't say that.

Or say that she were an evolutionist/atheist; she would then have to realize that she would be going against the grain of natural selection. Procreation is the principle that natural selection rests upon. Without it, natural selection would be moot – irrelevant, non-existent.

Too many times this is used: abortion to 'correct,' if you will, one's actions. It's hard to accept the consequences of one's actions. Roe v. Wade made a way to avoid the consequences.

I fervently believe life begins at conception. Being that I have at best minimal access to the legal system, I read Roe v. Wade and its progeny (no pun intended). A debate is established on when life begins. How can it be that one would believe that it begins at birth? It's moving inside the mother – has a beating heart – but people can still say that it isn't human until it is born.

The irony is that legislatures could not prosecute someone for the death of that baby when caused by assault. The Supreme Court said it wasn't human so you can't argue that a crime was committed. Strangely, I recently read about such cases going forth. Does the contradiction come to light?" (2-16-00).

Believing that Joe's questions were valid and his conclusions thoughtfully made, I wrote a brief response in my next letter:

"In your last letter, you were decrying abortion, and you pretty well expressed my sentiments. I believe abortion is very much like the holocaust in Europe in the 1930s and 1940s. Our society has awarded women the <u>legal</u> right to abortion on demand. But they do not have a <u>moral</u> right! God surely calls it murder, and it surely is unnatural!

If you have a chance, try to get the book entitled *Lifeviews* by R.C. Sproul. The publisher is Fleming H. Revell, a division of Baker Book House Co. Sproul speaks to the topic of abortion rights in Chapter 7." (2-27-00).

Obviously we were like-minded regarding our views on abortion, but we continued to grapple with the underlying concerns associated with mandated death penalties. These issues came to a head in 2008 with some executions that Joe knew about and shared with me.

"Wednesday the 21st we had an execution. Ulysses was his name. He had a date set back in October, but it was stayed because the Supreme Court wanted to deal with the lethal injection question. Once that was out of the way, that opened the door for Ulysses to have a new date set. The attorney general (A.G.) here was being contrary because he asked the state Supreme Court to set the date for May 5th, which was Ulysses' birthday. What was worse was that the executions in __occur on Wednesdays, but the 5th is a Monday. He knew it was a sorry request but would not remain above the dumb stuff.

We waited all day in our cells for word to come down. On the day one happens it's a lockdown, so we have little to do but sit and think of what he's going through and what we are very much likely to as well. They pronounced him dead at 6:15. Then for days we got to hear all this nonsense about how it wasn't carried out swiftly enough and that it cost too much. Dave, they had killed him, he had paid the price, and yet they still weren't satisfied. I hated how no one was looking at how a man was killed. No one would shut up and think that the punishment demanded was carried out. It was pure greed involved.

To make matters worse, the A.G. said he plans to conduct three more executions before the year is out. The most in a year since I've been here is two. Ulysses made the 5th person killed but the 9th death-row prisoner killed total in the time I've spent here. Two were stabbed to death, one was beat to death and one hung himself.

Lots of talk of speeding the process of appeals up. Lots of forgetfulness that 2 months ago a man was let off death row an innocent man. The state medical examiner had given false testimony." (5-29-08).

Though this was not the first time Joe had mentioned executions, it was the first to include such a vivid description of the procedure. I wondered if Joe knew of Ulysses' crime, so I responded with some questions.

"Your account of the day Ulysses was executed was most profound. I tried to imagine how you and the others were feeling as you waited in lockdown: thinking of the mechanics of the procedure, the aftermath of the execution (talk, speculation, etc.), projecting to the time of your own execution (should it happen) and perhaps questions about justice, fairness, etc. You did not mention what Ulysses was convicted of doing, whether or not he was guilty and, if he killed another person, how that victim might have felt before and during that execution. Is it fair for me to ask about Ulysses' victim or was Ulysses' execution just about Ulysses?

You also mentioned 'forgetfulness that 2 months ago a man was let off death row an innocent man. The state medical examiner had given false testimony.' Can you answer these questions for me?

1. What should happen to the M.E. for committing perjury?
2. Was the man released truly innocent? Are these fair, relevant questions?" (7-5-08).

Joe's quick response indicated that he understood the reasons for my questions about Ulysses. It helped me to know that he understood my concern for Ulysses' victim(s) and our joint concerns for the fate of a perjuring medical examiner.

"You had some questions about Ulysses and his execution. He was convicted of killing a woman that had left her church. I don't remember what the underlying felony was that made it capital murder. Yes, it is fair to ask about the victim. That's the point of all of it in the first place. I was complaining that once the sentence was carried out, there was no recognition that justice had been done – only a greedy desire to kill. And really, had justice been done? Just because a sentence was carried out that doesn't mean justice was served. How many people learned what kind of man Ulysses had become since then?

We are to have another execution next week. This man doesn't deny his involvement, even asked to die, but he's not the one that actually did the killing. The one that did do it only got Life Without Parole, and the third defendant was set free. How does justice get served if the one more culpable gets a less sentence especially when he had not the remorse of the one to be executed?

And the one that was released from death row was in fact innocent. DNA evidence proved that he and his co-defendant had not committed the crime. The original suspect was matched to the murder and confessed to it.

The M.E. that committed perjury should have his medical license revoked and should have to do time just like he made others falsely imprisoned. If the system is to have legitimacy, then those that enforce the law must be held accountable to that law." (7-18-08).

In Joe's next letter, less than two weeks later, he reported another execution.

"Since I last wrote we had another execution. Alvin B. was his name. I hadn't spent much time around him until the last few months. He was a cool dude but crazy looking.

A few days before the execution, the governor pardoned a man after serving 19 years for murder. We had hoped the governor would do something for Alvin because he had not actually killed anyone. He had been involved, but his co-defendant was the one that did the killing. Alvin got death while his co-defendant got life without parole.

The governor wasn't interested in that logic. The other notable thing about his case was the speed it moved. It was ten years from trial to execution. They have been setting the system up to move faster, and this is one such example of their success. I'd be dead three years now if that had happened to me.

Before Alvin left he gave me two envelopes of song lyrics that he had written down. I was surprised that he would do that. They were a personal item, and I would not have expected that he would give them to me or that he had such a favorable opinion of me that he would even think of me.

It was another crazy night to sit in my cell and know that he was going through and be able to look over and see those envelopes.

I'm not sure but there may be another before the year is out. There are to be three or more next year. I so need to get out of this place; please keep us all in your prayers." (9-2-08).

When I responded later that month, I decided to try to connect Alvin's recent demise to a project that was awaiting me. My hope was to temper the stark reality of an execution with a look at the potential spiritual dimension that believers could anticipate:

"In two weeks, beginning October 6, I will be teaching a class here at the conference center where I live. It is called 'Glimpses of Heaven.' I will be sharing some glimpses of what others have written and believe about those of us who are heaven-bound. You may know that God has not fully revealed the realities of heaven, but instead, gives us only glimpses. Yet, these have served to whet my appetite and support the hope I have for eternal life with Him. I hope that <u>your hope is the same</u>! Most of what I will share comes from the book, *Glimpses Of Heaven,* compiled by Richard Leonard and JoNancy Sundberg, published by Howard Books in 2007.

In light of these ideas, may I ask you: in your opinion, what is the status of Alvin B. regarding the after-life? In my last letter to you (July 5). I mentioned *Luke 16:19-31,* Jesus' clear rendering of the heaven-hell dichotomy awaiting all humans. Did Alvin ever share with you about his spiritual life (or lack thereof)? Did you ever take (make) an opportunity to share about your own hope? Did his song lyrics speak of hope or despair? You and I have been corresponding for almost nine years. Throughout, my goal has been to tell you of eternal life *(John 3:16)*, of acknowledgment and confession of sins, of receiving God's forgiveness through the death and resurrection of His Son and of receiving His promise (and our hope) of eternal life. Perhaps you can find ways of sharing this Good News with others facing execution and eternity." (9-23-08).

The following month, Joe commented on some of my questions about Alvin B. Obviously, he and Alvin had had some discussions regarding their religious beliefs; and he admitted some uncertainties about his spiritual concerns.

"You asked me several questions about Alvin and his stance with God. Ultimately the questions revolve around my own faith. B. was fully aware of the claims of the Bible. He chose a different religion. His eternity will be judged by God. Did B. share his religious stance with me? No, we had not been near to one another to get that kind of rapport. And when we did, we didn't talk religion. I felt he had a reasonable grasp of what the Bible said and that he was set in what he believed. And I didn't tell him of my faith. I have had a problem of not being able to live up to 1 Peter 3:15b.* That

---

* 'Always be prepared to give an answer to everyone who asks to give the reason for the hope that you have.'

was why I brought it up in the last letter, and why the new year resolution was so important this year. I needed to be familiar with what I claim to believe. So my own 'hope' rests on shaky ground. I'm trying to make up for that with the reading. Sharing the Good News doesn't feel right when I don't feel infused with the Good News when I'm so ignorant of it. I've played around, and I'm not happy about it. I'm trying to change that; kinda like Matthew 7:1-5. Get a grasp of it before you try to tell others about it." (10-7-08).

In late 2009, I wrote Joe and asked about his latest appeal; and I mentioned a recent event at Fort Hood in Texas that had captured national headlines. The tragedy brought us again to our ongoing discussions about dealing with murder and murderers.

"The appeals process moves very slowly, doesn't it? Our legal system creates much uncertainty; we seldom seem to know if we ever get our verdicts right (correct). In that regard, what is your opinion of the Army major who allegedly massacred a dozen people at Fort Hood last week? What should our society do to (with, for) him?" (11-09).

In early 2010, Joe wrote this thoughtful reply:

"You had asked what I thought of the major that had killed all those people at Fort Hood. What should be done with him? I was worried about how he was treated at first. People rarely act to do something from no provocation. I didn't like how he was a Muslim and his fellow soldiers felt like messing with his head, being cruel. The soldier is there to protect the country and the rights incumbent in that country. That means all of them are to protect a person's right to freedom of religion. If a soldier won't let another person practice their faith without harassment, then what is it that they stand for?

Now, I'm not saying that he shouldn't be punished for the crimes. He did them, but culpability really needs to be judged in context of what created the scenario. Should he be put to death? No. He's a lost soul, a Muslim. He needs people to get to him to let him experience the God we worship. We have to find a way to touch him to bring him from the depths of his separation from God. God doesn't give up on us, why would we give up on others? I don't like the idea that people will discard others so easily. This Chuck Colson book, How Now Shall We Live, has given me a more personal understanding of how to treat others. People foul up. They do so badly, but God still loves us, and we should do our bit to pass that on. Colson said that Christians are doing two things: either we are making the earth a worse place – hades on earth, or making it a better place – a heaven on earth. We have to try to do the latter." (2-4-10).

Joe wrote again in March and in April. In his letter of April 21, 2010, he spoke of two major concerns. The first of these was that he was running out of appeals. He put it this way:

> "I had my latest appeal filed on the 8th. This is the important one. I absolutely need relief here or it's all over with. We were only able to raise one issue, but have asked the court to hear two more. I'm still very confident in John's work, even with the loss of the last appeal. He's a great lawyer."

Before he ended this letter, he returned to the latest plans for executions, the other concern:

> "I need you to put someone on your prayer list – at home and church. Actually it's three names. Things are very bleak with the prospects of success with their cases, and I fear execution dates will soon be in the picture. The attorney general has already requested such for one.
>
> Their names are: Marvin Jamison, Jerry Morris and Jim Bob Butler. They need the prayers. Thanks." (4-21-10).

Joe's concerns quickly materialized, for my next mailing from him contained two essays. The cover page for the first read thusly: JERRY MORRIS, An essay by Harry Joseph Prescott, 4 pages, approx. 850 words, May 2010. This essay is at Appendix B. The other cover page read: JIM BOB BUTLER, An essay by Harry Joseph Prescott, 3 pages, approx. 730 words, May 2010. This essay is at Appendix C.

These tributes reveal some of Joe's deepest feelings about most of the issues covered in this chapter, and they initiated what would be one of our stormiest exchanges. Please read both essays before considering the remainder of this chapter.

I appreciated what he had written but perhaps was too critical in my initial response. Here's how it played out in the ensuing months:

"I want to respond to your last two letters: essays regarding two executions.

> Both had a sad, somber tone and perhaps a bit of incredulity along with a lack of care and concern for the victims. You said about Jerry: 'I didn't want to kick it with people I couldn't become friends or care about them because that would make their deaths more difficult to contend with. Be dispassionate became my rule.' Do you think Jesus emulates such unconcern? Is this the sort of attitude you'd recommend for yourself by your pen pals, family and other death-row inmates? Isn't this the attitude that you feel ___ has as you call it a 'killing machine?' Help me here, Joe. Am I misunderstanding something? Wouldn't a fellow-inmate do well to try to be a compassionate friend to one about to die? Wouldn't a Christian try to share the Gospel with one who is about to die and, perhaps, spend his eternity in hell?

> Later, you described your mind 'exchanging the pronouns – not he but I have two hours... Good God, I don't want to die.' Of course you don't!

But what about Jerry's victim(s)? Did Jerry have a victim? If so, did his victim want to die? Was he given a chance to live? Do you care? Should you care?

When we look at a situation, no matter how tragic and/or traumatic, only from our own perspective, we are being decidedly one-sided and selfish.

Joe, if it's possible to see anything positive, even perhaps redeeming, about these two executions, I believe both men did all they could to 'right' very wrong and tragic situations. Again I quote from your essay (assuming your information is correct): 'He (Morris) repeated the Lord's Prayer and asked for forgiveness... He asked that his body be released to the University Medical Center in ___.' God requires that we acknowledge and repent our sins; that's the only way we can be forgiven. And Jerry's gift of his body for medical research could potentially help another live longer, etc. That being the case, why were you compelled to say, 'Some medical student will continue the tradition of learning dissection with a criminal's body'? It seems to me that Jerry made a magnanimous gift, a fitting, final measure of grace and compassion.

'He (Butler) recites Psalm 23, asks for forgiveness, and says he's sorry.' What finer things could he have said?

Well, on to other things. You may think me to be a raving, capital punishment nut. If so, you're wrong! On the other hand, I cannot abide a two (or more)-sided situation being reduced to only one side. I hope you understand my points." (7-1-10).

Almost three months passed before I heard from Joe. I had wondered if I had been too strong in trying to make my points as I reacted to his two essays, and I was concerned that I had sullied our long-standing pen-pal relationship. His next letter straightened me out – big time!

"Two months have passed since I got your last letter. I broke my monthly writing schedule to you because your letter left my emotions roiling. I couldn't focus my thoughts. You left me angry and sad and lost.

It's been 11 years now we have been writing and it seems we don't really know one another.

You wrote, 'Both had a sad, somber tone and perhaps a bit of incredulity along with a lack of care and concern for the victims.' In response to the two essays you wrote that? Of course they were sad and somber – people are being killed and there's no care or concern about the 'victims' of state-sanctioned murder. Yes, there's some incredulity – how is it that I am supposed to care but no one else does?

As for the state's victims – I did care; do care. With someone that has the schooling and training and extensive ministry to prisoners, I don't know how you don't see a classic example of a defense mechanism. I didn't want to kick it with people or become friends. I had to become dispassionate because whether I like it or not this place is painful. It hurts to be here. It's miserable dreadful. And to make friends with people that you are likely to watch go to their deaths eviscerates what little sanity is left.

You were quick to point out my unconcern. God, I don't understand you. How do you miss it? I admit that my writings are not genius material or even remotely scholarly. In fact, I get most times simple and concise as the common description. But to read some of my stuff, you only have to scratch the surface to see more.

Be dispassionate became my rule. You espouse that as evidence of my unconcern. Didn't you recognize that I had to work at that? Didn't you see the opposite had to be true in order to create the rule? I never could be fully dispassionate. It was–is–a rule that I've frequently broken. I care so very much that I write these essays to tell people about those guys and send them out to everyone that might care.

Ironically, not many people do care. But I'm the one charged with shouldering the care, or I'm some sort of sociopath. Pen pals quit writing behind the essays; they couldn't handle or didn't care.

How much prison ministry have you done? You asked, 'Wouldn't a Christian try to share the Gospel with one who is about to die and perhaps spend his eternity in hell?' People are jaded about Christianity. Imagine wanting a relationship with God and every chaplain or preacher that comes through is a staunch supporter of your death. I don't want to hear that nonsense! Go away!

You wrote in one of your essays, 'we humans thrive on hope.' Really? Ain't that something. I'm hoping and praying that I don't have to make that walk and then a man of God comes to my door to ask when my date is, why did it take so long to reach.

We don't talk to one another like that here; it has no traction. We do try to be good to one another as best we can. And frequently there is not the full-blown version of Christianity that you've had decades to develop, but there is a flowering of it. That's why the guys at the end repeated the Lord's Prayer or Psalms 23. Other men here mean no harm. The best I can do is hope God will accept these crushed and useless men.

Where's your reasoning when it comes to Jerry's and Jim Bob's victims? You want me to comment on them, express concern or care. How do I do that with someone I never met or had an emotional connection to? Yeah, it's horrible that someone died, but I'm so far removed from the fact that it actually has no import. You would have me concerned if your neighbor down the road died but not for you. I don't know them; I know you.

Your sentence, 'Again I quote from your essay (assuming your information is correct)...' What is that? Why did you throw that jab in there? Assuming I'm correct or wrong, are you?

Why did I end Jerry's essay with 'some medical student will continue the tradition of learning dissection with a criminal's body'? I recognized the value and generosity Jerry was doing by donating his body, but no one else did. No, all anyone wanted was to <u>use</u> him some more. In fact, I would bet you a hundred dollars that people were saying to speed up executions so as to use more bodies for research. Next thing they'll champion harvesting organs. Never with the mindset that someone was trying to do something that one last time but for their greedy agendas.

The death penalty is a tool, not for justice, but for political advancement. They use us from the very beginning; and, even in Jerry's last 'magnanimous gift' they had only designs in using him.

I'm amazed at your apparent desire for a one-sided situation. Especially since that is exactly how we always operate. We never have complete information on any given situation. We always make decisions with a decidedly one-sided bent.

And I don't sense once that you might have questioned the necessity of killing those men. Surely a multi-sided approach would have asked whether or not their deaths were necessary. Was justice served? You do realize that justice has no application in our legal system, don't you?

I wrote about Lofton when he was executed and noted a complete lack of response on the topic from you. Everyone from the Attorney General, Governor, even to the jurors knew he was not the actual killer. They knew he was there and was involved but was not the killer. His co-defendant was. Yet Lofton got the death penalty and was subsequently executed. His co-defendant got life without parole. Wanna tell me where justice is?

Or Marvin Jamison who was executed in July. His co-defendant, Phil, knew the victim, introduced Marvin to him, suggested robbing him, participated in the murder and robbery and bragged for months that he had killed someone. But when he was arrested, he blamed it all on Marvin. He snitches, gets a reduced sentence and testifies against Marvin, who gets the death penalty and is executed. Then Phil is paroled after 12 years. You got some justice in there for me?

That one hurts, because Marvin had become a friend. He told me he had done the crime with Phil, and he felt horrible for years. He said he never would have been involved but for meth that had him tweaked out. The repentant gets to die while the gloater goes on.

I don't care whether you think I'm innocent or not. Don't you get it – truth does not matter. The U.S. Supreme Court has said that claims of actual innocence will not be entertained <u>unless</u> there is a constitutional violation first. So, if you do not have such a violation, then you don't get to argue that you are innocent. And even if you might have one, the court can argue that it was harmless error and still never reach the merits of your innocence. How's that for one-sided?

I got several responses from the essays I sent out. You were the most hard core. There was one that expressed a profound sadness and stated no matter one's sins we must show kindness and compassion to them. I don't get that from you – the only vibe I really get is your adherence to Romans 13, never considering it is a conditional adherence.

I'll write more tomorrow." (9-21-10).

I waited two weeks, anticipating that Joe would have some more rebuke for me, then I decided to respond. Here is my letter of October, 2010:

> "You have thoroughly chastised me; and, to the extent that I deserve it, I thank you.

> In my last letter, my intent was not to offend either you or the memory of Jerry Morris and Jim Bob Butler. Rather, I was trying to be an advocate for their victims. And I realize that you didn't know them, but to not mention them suggests to me that you don't realize that they had family members, friends, etc. who experienced similar feelings to those of yours when Morris and Butler were executed. If your feelings matter, so do theirs!

> In our years of pen-paling, I have tried to remind myself and you of God's influence in my life and my reliance on His Word (the Bible) for wisdom and direction in my life. I have sensed that you, too, are wanting to be dependent upon God. I want to give you a passage to check out: 'Do not be deceived: God cannot be mocked. A man reaps what he sows. The one who sows to please his sinful nature, from that nature shall reap destruction; the one who sows to please the Spirit, from the Spirit will reap eternal life' (Galatians 6:7-8). These verses are relevant to our discussion, so I want to comment and invite your response.

Using an agricultural metaphor, Paul is telling us that when we sow sin, we should expect to reap destruction. What will this destruction be? Here are some possibilities: a destroyed name (reputation), a destroyed family, a destroyed life (physical death) and/OR eternal damnation (spiritual death). What have you reaped (what are you reaping) from your sins?

King David committed adultery with Bathsheba, impregnated her and, to try to cover it all, had her husband killed (that's murder). You may read this sordid story and its sad aftermath in 2 Samuel 11-24. David reaped much pain and sorrow for the remainder of his life <u>because of his sins</u>.

BUT... God has some great, Good News for us! First, note the word OR (capitalized above) – here's why: Because of our sins we will reap certain consequences including physical death, but God has provided a Way for us not to die spiritually. The WAY is Jesus (read John 14:5-6)

Now read Luke 23:32-43. Jesus saved the repentant criminal just before he died on the cross (verse 42 – I believe we've discussed this passage previously). Along with you, I hope He did the same for Jerry and Jim Bob and Marvin Jamison, who 'felt terrible for years' (for being an accomplice of Phil's in a murder). Perhaps his horrible feeling was tantamount to repentance, and perhaps God forgave his sin and called him to eternal life.

Some of your assessments of our judicial system are likely accurate. All human entities are imperfect and make mistakes. Mistakes made intentionally are unconscionable; those made unintentionally are unfortunate. Interestingly, Joseph's story in the Old Testament and Paul's story in the New Testament are examples of the former type of mistake. Since you have been reading through the Bible (more than once), you have already read these accounts. If you wish to review them, read Genesis 37 and 39-50 for Joseph's plight and the book of Acts for Paul's situations. Because God was overseeing it all (as He is overseeing your life and mine), Romans 8:28 applies to both men, to me and, I trust, to you.

Back to our judicial system: through my adult years, I have served on five or six jury panels. I discovered how difficult it is to determine guilt or innocence ('beyond a reasonable doubt' or 'based upon a preponderance of the evidence'). Only God and the guilty criminal knows for sure if the accused is guilty or innocent. That fact, in itself, ought to show why jurors and judges have such difficulty. When you add to that other factors: (1) most accused, whether guilty or innocent, claim to be not-guilty; (2) some witnesses (particularly those who have committed the crime with an accomplice) try to put all the guilt on the accomplice. Wasn't that the case with Phil and Jamison? You called it 'snitching.' (3) other witnesses try to give evidence (untrue or unknown) to protect an accused, it's easy to see how truth in a case is hard to determine.

Joe, have you ever been involved in a court proceeding (as a witness or a juror) other than at your own trial? If so, you may understand why jurors' and judges' tasks are difficult. Nevertheless, the law says we must hear the evidence and render a verdict – hoping that the decision is correct.

I re-read the letter I sent you in July; I recant nothing! You took issue with my comment, 'assuming your information is correct.' It was not intended as a jab; rather it was questioning your confidence in information received and its source. Let me be specific: in your last letter you wrote, 'We never have complete information on any given situation.' Two paragraphs later, you wrote:

> 'I wrote about Lofton when he was executed and noted a complete lack of response on the topic from you. Everyone from the Attorney General, Governor, even, to the jurors knew he was not the killer. His co-defendant was. Yet, Lofton got the death penalty and was subsequently executed while his co-defendant got LWOP. Wanna tell me where the justice is?'

I question how you knew that 'everyone' knew that he was not the actual killer. Please don't be incensed with the question; just tell me how you knew.

When a person commits a crime, an atrocious crime, what would be the very best outcome for that person, for the victim(s) and for society? In other words, how would justice (getting what is deserved) best be served? Here are some possible answers:

1. Find a way to restore the criminal to society, so that he becomes a responsible, productive member. He is grateful to be restored, and he never again commits a crime.
2. Put the criminal away from society (incarcerate him for life without parole). This insures safety for society and its members, but it's expensive.
3. Eliminate the criminal from society (execution). This is society's most effective deterrent (but for that criminal only, for it does not deter others from committing atrocities).

If I answered my own question raised above, I would say the first answer is the best – hands down! So, what's wrong with it? The main problem is that criminals are not easily restored; the current recidivism rate is 75 percent. With such a dismal success rate, is it a surprise that society is reluctant to give heinous criminals another chance to kill, maim, destroy, etc? Whose fault is it that most criminals, returned to society, become repeat offenders?

So, Joe, I have brought several sides to the issues of crimes, criminals, victims, judicial decisions, etc. All sides are important!

You wrote, 'You do realize that justice has no application in our legal system, don't you?' Justice means <u>getting what one deserves</u>. So, what do you mean 'has no application?' Do you mean justice <u>does</u> not apply or justice <u>should</u> not apply? Think of justice as discipline. The Bible says, God disciplines those whom He loves. This is just like a human father who disciplines his child to obtain right (proper) behavior. I argue that it most certainly does have application. However, both mercy (not getting what one deserves) and grace (getting what one does not deserve) have application as well. Our God is a God of justice, mercy and grace!

You wrote, 'I don't care whether you think I'm innocent or not. Don't you get it – truth does not matter.' What a tragic conclusion you have reached! It makes me feel that all of our letter-exchanging has been in vain, because I agreed at the outset to write only if you would be honest with me... As for your assertion that 'truth does not matter,' you couldn't be more wrong! God is Truth; His Son is Truth! Satan is a liar and a murderer!

If you choose to write me again, in light of our disagreements, why don't you tell me what you think you deserve from society and why. And, if you receive from society what you deserve, what does society have a right to expect from you in return?" (10-5-10).

Almost six weeks passed before I received Joe's next letter. He felt that he owed me at least one more round of comments. While neither of us knew when, and if, we would finally "bury the hatchet," we both realized that we had come too far to quit corresponding. As it turned out, his following letter would be the last to address the capital punishment issue; more pressing matters were soon to come:

"I missed last month in writing to you, but I will make sure to get this out to you tonight.

I have to point out that I do not want to stop this correspondence. We have issues we disagree about, but I do not feel that is reason to not write. I will not agree for the sake of convenience.

You are again an advocate for victims you did not know. You did aggravate me with this, '... to not mention them suggests to me that you don't realize that they had family members...' Why do you equate the not mentioning them with an ignorant, callous mentality on my part? Of course I knew they had family. Of course I knew that there were victims. The rule for writers is write what you know. I knew the guys that were executed.

At what point did you think that maybe these guys don't need to be murdered by the state? Or do you feel that regardless of how repentant and deeply sorry people are – kill 'em all? Do you think that everyone on death row needs to be killed? Yes or no? How many people have you known from death row? How many of them across the country do you feel are innocent? You do know that there have been more than 100 people released from death row that have been found to be innocent? To me, society should be shutting this death machine down for good. It has a high rate of abuse.

And I'm not that sympathetic to juries and judges having a hard time with their roles. It should be so. The more flippant people are about it, the more abuses are generated.

Pay attention to the decision likely to come out of the U.S. Supreme Court this year. The DA's office in Louisiana put an innocent man in prison. He got out and tried to sue, but the DA has absolute immunity. So he tried to sue through the DA's staff. They withheld information about his innocence. They intentionally put an innocent man in prison. You were fond of pointing out that we reap what we sow; what do you think the DA's office should reap for falsely convicting and imprisoning people? Why does every area of our government have a checks and balance system, but the DA has absolute free reign?

'All human entities are imperfect and make mistakes. Mistakes made intentionally are unconscionable; those made unintentionally are unfortunate.' Believe that, do you? If you reason that we are so, then don't you suspect that we have no business exacting such a toll as the death penalty? Why reason that people will make mistakes, they will foul up (in some cases very, very bad), but be undeterred in an absolute punishment?

It's little consolation to the innocent person being killed that 'well... you know the system is imperfect and makes mistakes.' Knowing it makes mistakes, our system should reflect that. Absolute punishment from an imperfect system dealing with imperfect people is beyond absurd.

How did I know that all relevant parties knew Lofton was not the actual killer? They, themselves, stated so. Whether via news, point, or legal brief, each was aware that Lofton was not the most culpable person. You challenged this aspect as if it couldn't happen!

You totally missed my point about truth. You don't even remotely understand. I'm firmly aware of truth and its application. I was arguing that society is not concerned with truth – that it does not matter there. As a sociologist, you must be aware of postmodernism and its stance on truth. Since society is not concerned for truth, then it operates from a vantage that injustices committed are not needed to be corrected. From a vantage that injustices really don't occur since truth must be understood in order to determine what response should follow. Truth only matters to those that actually want it!

It's funny that you point out a 75 percent recidivism rate. I don't believe it's that high, but it doesn't matter. You want to know who's ultimately responsible for this – society or the criminal? Society! A person is groomed from childhood by society that we evolved from monkeys, that there is no objective truth, that morality is antiquated and of no use to modern man, that any mistakes people make should be corrected by suing people in court.

When people act the way they do, it's because they were taught so. People do not grow up apart from society; society is the womb. If someone were polite and mannerly and responsible, you'd say that was good upbringing. Why does the opposite not exist?

Why is it 75 percent? If you were to come to this prison, you would find very little in the way of rehabilitation. The system is not designed to put people back out there. It's designed to house people in order to make money off them. That's what the private prison industry is all about. They can't make money if people are being rehabilitated and put on the path of good civil, constructive citizens. It's why private prisons lobby for stricter, longer sentences. It's why people have to be tough on crime.

It's a shame that Jesus can fully recognize us as flawed, accept us into His arms when we repent and wash the old crime away, but you as the follower of Jesus cannot.

I'm not gonna stop writing to you because we don't agree. I figure we've given too many years writing together without a sufficient challenge of our beliefs.

Thanksgiving is this week, and I wish you, Deanna and the boys all a happy one. Please take care, be good and remember, we all are flawed." (11-21-10).

After debating these heavy issues for 11-12 years, I suppose Joe and I reached a mutually-acceptable truce. But the profound questions of life and death remained for our continuing struggle:

- Are we really "our brothers' keepers?"
- Is restoration really possible for capital offenders?
- How many times should we forgive one who has sinned against us?

- Are "correctional" facilities, in reality, only "custodial" facilities?
- After God's example, can we be persons of justice <u>and</u> mercy <u>and</u> grace?

CHAPTER 6

The Beginning
of the End

Earlier (in Chapter 4) I spoke of Joe's mention that his end might be approaching. I return now to that theme – to supplement and enhance those conversations given earlier.

Following the devastating loss of his final appeal, Joe experienced both remorse and depression. In July, 2011, he wrote of these feelings, but I sensed that an upswing of his indomitable spirit had begun. That mood swing was contagious, so in August I wrote to encourage his resumption of activities that had served him so well throughout his incarceration.

> "You are doing well to resume your daily schedule of writing, yard time and trusty duties. This is mentally healthy for you, because when you are involved in these activities you cannot easily dwell on depressing matters and 'what-if giants.' I urge you to place all of this turmoil and uncertainty in God's hands. You do this through prayer, and you ask those who love you to intercede in your

behalf – to God and later to the governor. Deanna and I pray regularly for you, and we will continue to do so. We will trust you and others to help us know what else to do and when." (8-29-11).

In September Joe was continuing to vacillate in thoughts and actions. He wrote on the twenty-first:

"Today has been my upswing. I have been on some miserable lows. I should be doing worse because my appeal was filed on the 19th in the U.S. Supreme Court. That means from here on out I am on borrowed time. My upswing really resides in the fact that I spent the morning obsessively organizing and cleaning my cell. We were told to pack up Monday so that the painting crews could come in. All my stuff is packed when a shakedown comes. They ransack my property so that half is packed and half is spread out. It's a disorganized mess. Yesterday we were waiting on word if we could move or if we could unpack. It turns out that we will be moving but not yet. This morning I tackled my organized spirit and got to work. I am back in order, so I wrote this journal entry: 'I am stupidly organized.' I mean I have done it up right and obsessively so. That has made me feel so much better. I rationalize this fanatic aspect of me because I think it is really the result of no control. My cell is absolutely in my control and therefore my responsibility.

I have written few letters this month; even fewer got started and never completed. Depression has always been described as having a lack of desire for the things you like to do or normally do. I've felt I was in some sort of depression, but it hit me hard in August. I crashed! I couldn't motivate myself; I lost interest, and I couldn't fight it. I was – and still am – in a sort of fugue; a funk. It's constricting – suffocating – me!

Please pray that your letter is my rebound, my embracing of my manic writing and activities." (9-21-11).

At the end of this letter, Joe shared an interesting experience. He seemed to make light of this encounter, but to me it seemed particularly demoralizing at this time in his life's journey. Surely this is not indicative of the rank-and-file of clerics who make visits in our correctional facilities around the country. I surely hope not!

"Ha! Let me tell you... We had this huge group of chaplains come on the tier – cattle to a slaughter, it looked like. But they had the fire of the Lord! They wanted to convert. Yeah, weren't serious; they were too comfortable in their niches in life. I told them I could be executed in December or January. Do you know they left my door!? They ran! Where's the Lord now? I know where He is, of course. But they were not committed to the cause near as much as they thought. It reminds me of the topic my friend, Charles, and I have discussed several times. We believe that Americans need a bit of persecution – as Christians. They don't appreciate the faith in a visceral sense. It's easy to drive to church in your nice new truck wearing your Sunday best with those fake societal smiles on. It's quite another to actually attest one's faith in very troubling, even abusive, times. Would you agree that those that profess, but have never been really tested, are the ones that Jesus will say, 'I never knew you; go away?'

I'm not trying to be mean, but I am trying to point out a flaw in some people's commitment value." (9-21-11).

Joe wrote again in November; he was continuing to fight for his life, but he was hitting dead ends and growing in desperation. How difficult it must have been to try to sustain a battle while incarcerated with minimal tools and communication. In such a fight, one is almost totally dependent on the good will of allies outside the prison walls. If one has an idea for a strategy, how long does it take to get this to one's lawyers or other advocates? And all along, time is of the essence! I could sense the growing frustration and terror in his letter:

"Not sure where I should start – I will though select September. I had been working on some projects hoping to be able to fight this some way, somehow. I was eager to go to the visits with my attorneys on the first. Enthusiasm was actually something I had again. But it wasn't long after I got there that they had kicked my enthusiasm in the teeth. I felt awful – wrung out. I came back to my cell and laid out on the floor and tried to sleep some of the misery away. I woke with a resolve to accept what I could not fight. I gathered up a big pile of my property in the center of my cell and then gave it all away. The guys I gave it to recognized my mindset. Everyone that has had to make that walk has done the same thing. I just did it a little earlier, but it didn't help my mood.

What made it worse was the news of Johnny Forsyth's execution in Georgia. I had read about him for years; he had had a huge following and yet they still were not able to stop the state from killing him. What right did I have thinking I could make it?

The only reason I've somewhat come out of this funk is the state asked for a continuance in my case. Their brief, in opposition to mine filed before the U.S. Supreme Court, was due October 26th. They got an extension until November 28th. That means that I have been granted a month I had not calculated I would live. If the state files on time, the earliest the court would look at my appeal would be January 6. That means I would squeak by for my 35th birthday. I'm trying to use this spark to get to writing again." (11-21-11).

I felt Joe's growing uneasiness, and it affected me in kind. I was compelled to respond quickly and wanted to be upbeat and encouraging. I commented on the apparent rite of passage of collecting and giving away one's possessions to others, and I asked Joe to meditate on a passage in Luke's Gospel.

> "Hey! Good to hear from you. It seems that there is always something exciting going on in your unit; I guess it's so you all won't get bored! More on that later – did you have a good Thanksgiving: turkey, dressing, cranberry sauce, etc.?

> Now, back to the doings at your unit: you gave away a lot of your 'stuff,' the other guys were glad to receive it, but it didn't help your mood? So, will the guys give it back; or, if they try, will you take it back? I'm pleased that you got a continuance, but what is the latest on your request for some of us to write the governor?

> When you write again, please catch me up on the status of your appeal and expectations. None of us know 'how much longer the Lord wants one here.' In a sense, we're all living on borrowed time; but isn't it comforting to know that we're in the Lord's hands? He came to earth that first Christmas ultimately to die for our sins, so that we would be with Him for eternity. That's God's plan and God's Good News. When you can, read and meditate on Luke 12:1-12, especially verses 4 and 5. In this passage, Jesus is telling us what (who) to fear and who not to fear." (11-28-11).

In late February, 2012, I received Joe's last letter; it began this way:

"So, I begin this letter with a heavy heart. I had a visit yesterday with my friend, Charles. My mom, brother, and sister-in-law came in toward the end of the visit. They brought the news that the U.S. Supreme Court had declined to hear my case. I had prepared myself, and I was working to absorb the impact. I don't know that my family is as far along as I am. Later that night, the news announced that the state Attorney General had asked the state Supreme Court to set an execution date of March 21st.

Things have continued to fall apart, and I am struggling to hold on."

Following this announcement, Joe made three requests: (1) to ask the governor to commute his sentence to life without parole, (2) to sign a petition on line called 'Save Joe' and (3) to write a personal letter of recommendation in Joe's behalf.

Finally, Joe ended the letter with these thought-provoking comments:

"And then, it looks as if my death will be next month. You asked an obvious question about it being comforting to know that I was in the Lord's hands. The simple answer is the more comfortable I am depends on the better the relationship is. Lately that has been meager. Now I am having to abandon things that I have held onto. And I do believe that is making this better – the walk better. Yeah, I did move away from Him some. I never stopped believing, but I failed to make Him the center.

It doesn't take away the fear. Wow! That is still something else. It's there, but I refuse to let it overwhelm me, to take my drive away again.

The prayers of all those good people, including you, I believe have helped to keep me from veering too much off course.

I'm heaven-bound but still unsettled, still not completely committed to this walk. But I am getting my affairs in order. I wrote about giving a lot of my stuff away. You asked would the guys give it back. Yes, I do believe they would, but I would not ask for it back. Now the task is to give the rest of it away.

Dave, we have known one another for a very long time. You have been a mentor, friend, inspirer, and a brother-in-Christ. No matter what happens I am blessed to have been a part of your life. My gratitude can't be fully expressed, but I am deeply thankful for all you have done for me. It has been a pleasure to write and learn from you. Thank you so very much.

I need to close. Time is compressed, and there are a lot of other people I need to write. Please take care, stay outta trouble and, above all, thank you." (2-22-12).

Joe's situation was indeed dire; there seemed to be little time left to do anything. Deanna and I quickly signed his petition and wrote a letter to the governor. Then I felt an urgency to get a last letter off to Joe. What else could I say to him? Had I left any important stone unturned? Did he need comfort, or assurance, or hope, or advice? I realized that I had never before written to an about-to-die man – certainly not one in Joe's situation. God helped me remember one thing that I had never before mentioned. Here's how the letter unfolded:

> "Joe, I must write again now what I have tried to convey to you numerous times in the past: your <u>current</u> and <u>future</u> spiritual condition. If you feel that your worst-case scenario is your execution on March 21 (or some other date), you are wrong! Your worst-case scenario would be if, at your physical death, you were to translate to Satan's domain; it's called hell! I want you to be translated to God's domain; it's called heaven! More importantly, this is what God wants! Here's how heaven can be your destination:
>
> Heaven has nothing to do with the comment in your last letter, 'Yeah, I did move away from Him (God?) some. I never stopped believing but I failed to make Him the center.' Heaven has nothing to do with your being a Roman Catholic and attending Mass, nor does it have to do with me being a Southern Baptist, teaching Sunday school and singing in my choir.

Instead, heaven has to do with God's plan to save us. He has done this by providing for our sins to be forgiven. God's part was to offer His Son, Jesus, to die to pay the penalty for our sins. Our part is to confess our sins (all of them that we know about), turn away from them (repent) and thank Him for forgiving us. By accepting this gracious offer from God, we become righteous (justified in His eyes) and candidates for eternal life with Him in heaven.

This Good News (God's plan – the Gospel) is explained in a dozen different ways in the New Testament. I'd like to cite only one of these scriptures, because we have talked about it in previous letters. Do you remember the repentant thief crucified with Jesus, to whom Jesus said, 'Today, you will be with Me in Paradise" (Luke 23:39-43)?

Because you have insisted that you are innocent of murder, I must ask you this: what sin(s) did you commit in ____ at the home of ___? As you reflect on this question, you must recall Jesus' words in Matthew 5:27-30: these verses clearly tell us that our sinful <u>thoughts</u> (lust, intention to rob or kill, etc.) make us as guilty as if we actually did them! You know what these sins were, and God knows! Please, as you recall them, sincerely pray for forgiveness, and you will be forgiven – in

Jesus' name! If you've already done this, you need not do it again!

Then, please recall your sins while incarcerated. Have you fantasized about any illicit sexual behavior, have you been angry with others (correctional officers, fellow inmates, pen pals, etc.), have you cursed (aloud or to yourself) the courts, attorneys, judges, etc.? Please ask for forgiveness of these – in Jesus' name. If you are genuinely sincere, God will recognize and forgive you instantly!

Finally, I must remind you that our God has asked us to forgive others. Why shouldn't we forgive, if we expect to be forgiven? What I'm asking you to do may be one of the hardest things you've ever thought of doing. You testified in your trial (according to the account I read on-line) that you witnessed ____ murder his wife. That being true, I ask you to ask God to help you forgive ____ of that murder and for lying and allowing you to be convicted. Hopefully, one day ____ will confess murdering his wife. You would do well to ask God to convict him of his sin. Should that happen, can you imagine the joy of being reconciled with him in heaven?

We serve an awesome God for Whom nothing is too difficult, so before you dismiss what I am saying, please discuss all of this with God. Deanna and I are praying for your commutation

and for _____'s confession and your release. If none
of this happens, the joys of heaven await you!!!

With love and appreciation." (3-1-12).

The writer of the Epistle to the Hebrews said this: "Just as man
is destined to die once, and after that to face judgment, so Christ
was sacrificed once to take away the sins of many people; and He
will appear a second time, not to bear sin, but to bring salvation
to those who are waiting for Him" (9:27-28). After I wrote the
letter above, I was waiting for this promise to be manifested with
Joe. I did not hear about his execution, and I do not know the
date of his death. I harbor the hope that when my appointed time
to die comes, I will meet Joe, along with numerous other saints,
in heaven.

Ordinarily, then, this should be the conclusion of Joe's story;
but I was in for another surprise. Please read on.

AFTERWORD

Around the time that Joe's execution had been set, I received what really came to be his last letter. I was not expecting it, but how pleasing it was to see that he had received my last letter to him. And I'm pleased to share it here as a fitting end to his story. Joe, indeed, should have the last words!

> "This has been a long, wonderful correspondence. I am grateful, blessed to have known you. And I'm deeply thankful for the love and kindness and the fact that you've made me think.
>
> As I re-read your letter I am left with the desire to let the remaining stuff in me go. I don't know if other people do it, but I'm kinda hardheaded. I've held onto the things that really distracted the faith. I've veered off course. So the closer I get, the less junk I have in my head. This points out that I could have been doing this a long time ago. Hardheaded!
>
> You two have been so wonderful to me. I have had the pleasure to learn of God and the adventures you go on. You are such a vibrant couple. You've set the standard high – as it should be.
>
> I thank you for the letter of recommendation. The governor is looking at it as I write.

I won't talk of the points you made; you are right. I just want to make it known that you have shown me kindness and love that I never felt worthy of. Sometimes I would open your letter immediately; I knew that Dave was going to lay it on me – thankfully and rightly so. But I've never not had to think about what you wrote.

Tomorrow I go to Unit-17 where the executions occur. A part of me has sprung up to get the heck out of this flesh – my bane, my misery. Tuesday at 6:00 I'll go see God; I think I have some explaining to do!

Dave, Deanna, thank you from the bottom of my heart for your love. It has helped me through the misery. Joe." (3-17-12).

APPENDIX A

Sphexsophobia
By Harry Joseph Prescott

Even though it was still early in the day the temperature was well on its way to the triple digits. I could just start to see those heat vapors rising from the concrete outside my cell window. My cell is on the front of the building so I am able to see the inner workings of the unit. The whole prison is separated into units, each of a self-contained area housing varying amounts of prisoners.

This morning I am waiting on yard call as I look out at the officers and prisoners going about their tasks. The lawn crew is gearing up by doing maintenance on their different machines. I see one trustee start up a large Bush Hog. It isn't long before the breeze brings the scent of freshly cut grass to my nose.

There is a perimeter fence outside the building without the requisite razor wire. It's meant to be an added precaution in this maximum security unit to signify the even tighter security for the building, which is largely death row, of which I am a member.

The trustee has methodically cut until he has reached my building. The gate is open, he enters, and immediately turns left to cut along the fence. I can see the sweat and accumulation of dust on his face. The clanking diesel and whooshing blades are loud and clear.

He doesn't stay in my view long as he makes his initial cut. I quickly turn the knob on my window to block out the soon-to-arrive swirl of dust. The louvers just tighten down as I see the front of the tractor come back in view. I can tell by the way it shifts that its back left tire has dipped into a depression. The hole isn't deep enough to stop the tractor so it continues to cut.

He makes a complete circuit and then starts on the inner row. As he makes it back to the hole there is a sudden lurch of the tractor to the right and then screaming that is easily heard through the closed window.

I instantly recognize that the hole is an opening for a nest of yellow jackets that the tractor stirred up. They have viciously attacked the trustee and he has with all alacrity abandoned the tractor. He is flailing his arms, screaming and running all out to get away from the menace. He soon runs out of space due to the perimeter fence and with little hesitation scales and jumps it. Away he runs trying desperately to get some distance.

When the trustee lifted his foot off the gas the tractor stopped and idled. It had another safety feature so that if a driver ever rose off the seat the blades would stop spinning. An enormous swarm of yellow jackets has surrounded it, but stays back due to the diesel exhaust belting from it.

I have never seen so many yellow jackets in my life. There are easily thousands of them. They are angrily buzzing and bumping into my window screen. I am real glad they can't get to me.

Suddenly there is another loud scream, this time from a female officer. With a terrible dawning, I realize that she is inside the building. It doesn't take a rocket scientist to understand that someone has left the front door open; usually done to let fresh air circulate in. I hear the slam of the tower door and know that she has barricaded herself in it.

I jump from my bunk, above which the window is, and rush to the cell door. I thrust my mirror out to see my prediction of thousands as puny. My relief of how they could not get to me, dashed. There is a mass of them as thick and black and dangerous as a thunderstorm. There is no end in sight of this apocalyptical scourge.

The cells before me have been inundated and screaming, cussing, and frantic swatting erupts.

Trapped! All of us! We can't escape as the trustee and officer did.

I leap from the door to grab a sheet. I quickly tie it to the door to block them out but I'm too slow. I'm being stung as I desperately try to plug the cracks. I hear someone yell, "Help me! Help me!" as I stuff the last hole and slap at the little devils. It's no use to ask for help; you're on your own.

With the door blocked off I have now trapped many inside with me. I'm scared of them. I'm trying to save myself by spinning and swatting as many as I can. I can't make a dent in their numbers. "Good God, help me!" I voluntarily, hypocritically cry out.

One lands on my lip and I snap my mouth shut. I'm not aware of the force I am putting behind my slaps as I hit my left cheek. I stagger, crashing my right shoulder into the wall. It's bedlam! A thousandth of my size and they are soundly whipping me.

I don't know how long it took before I was able to get the upper hand. I had acquired the services of a rolled up newspaper that was pleasingly lethal. There are scores of little yellow and black bodies all around my feet. I have been stung numerous times, and I think how fortunate I am not to be allergic to them.

I usually only wear boxers in my cell and lately the heat has mandated it. This proved detrimental as it left huge areas of skin exposed for them to attack. I look myself over to see what appears to be a virulent case of chicken pox.

I am swatting at the remaining few when my attention is brought back to the tier at large. All bedlam has broken loose and I wonder if I could have lessened it by yelling a warning to those beyond me. I didn't think to yell out to them because I was so focused on blockading my door with the sheet. The swarm has encompassed the whole tier of 26 cells. It sounds like one of those hand-held vacuums held up to your ear – that high-pitched whining!

I think I am okay now. A lot of stings to contend with, but no more yellow jackets. Thank God!

My solace ends abruptly as the pestilence has gotten into the ventilation system. I am gripped with a viselike fear and my stomach suddenly feels hollow because they are coming, in hordes, through the vents. I grab a towel and jump from the toilet to the sink so I can reach the left-hand vent. I stuff it in halting that flank of wasps. This is only a half measure because the other vent is over the right-hand side of the door. This necessitates that I stand on the door; but if I do this, I pull the sheet down.

They are whaling me with a vengeance, but I am determined to fight on. I snatch up my cigarette lighter and grab a stack of old newspapers. I am breathing rapidly as I start a fire, twitching and squirming all the while. The fire is so slow in catching I agonize over the hoped- for relief. I know I can take it a little longer because this fire will be my salvation.

Mercifully it begins to roar and create a beautiful, sooty smoke. "Die, you devils!" I cry as I fan and feed the flames. My newest defense is working wonderfully and I let out a maniacal laugh. They are dropping like flies!

Reality then slaps me in the face as I begin to hack and cough. The smoke killed my adversaries and now has turned on me. I jump to my bunk to open my window, but there is no relief; the blowers are on meaning air is being sucked into the window but not blowing out. This, in turn, fans my fire creating even more smoke. I jump back down and promptly snuff it out. I am bouncing around like a ping pong ball.

I belatedly wrap another sheet around me to try to block the stings of any remaining wasps. I stagger unexpectedly and don't know why. My vision dims and I feel faint.

"Oh ___!" I may not be allergic but I'm going into anaphylactic shock anyway. Too many stings and my body's defense is shut down on me. I'm numb and can't continue to hold the sheet up. It falls to the floor where I trip on it falling down myself. The last thing I remembered was seeing the underside of my toilet, then blackness.

I don't know how long I was out. When I woke up I saw all white around me, but not the white of a hospital. It was the residue of a fire extinguisher. My sheet had been ripped from the door and my unconscious body sprayed to kill the last of the wasps.

My body aches all over, as if my muscles have recently had a strenuous workout. Saliva has pooled on the floor and dried to my cheek. My mouth tastes of the chemical spray. I push slowly off the floor to see the outline of the spray. I think I should be dead because it looks a lot – too much so – like a chalk line around a dead body.

I roll onto my butt to dumbly look around my cell. It's a mess of soot, charred paper, fire suppression and thousands of little yellow jackets. I push myself into a corner because I can hardly prop myself up any longer due to my weakness. I look at hundreds of nickel-size edematous sores all over me. It looks like someone has tortured me with a car's hot cigarette lighter.

The whole scary sequence of events replays itself in my head and I feel so tired, so weak, so beat. My head lulls back into the corner as I begin to cry. It's a deep, soul-rending cry that I can't control. My spirit is broken and all my long-buried emotions are rolling up to the surface.

I cried at the traumatic wasp invasion. I cried at how low people see me that I didn't warrant a trip to the hospital or any medical attention; none of us did. I cried at my miserable existence in prison. I cried at how I'll always be known as a murderer and can never redeem myself; can never show I'm a worthy person no matter what they say I did. I cried so hard and deeply that my sorrow had my chest constricted, leaving me gasping for air. The cry was so cathartic I could soon feel the release of years of tension and turmoil. I actually dozed off into a somewhat restful sleep afterwards. The venom still had a hold on me and sleep would be the best way to let it dissipate.

A while later I was roused by a trustee with a broom. He wanted to know if I wanted to sweep up the wasps in my cell. Life goes on! I was saddened that no medics had come to see us. I refused the use of the broom and got up to sore muscles not only from the effects of the stings but also from the uncomfortable sleeping position in the corner.

I slowly and gingerly cleaned up my cell. The wasps were dead but their stingers were still sharp. I gently scooped them up onto a cardboard dustpan and flushed them, along with the debris from the fire, down the toilet. Once completed I did a careful, minute examination of my body. Yellow jackets can sting repeatedly and not lose their stingers. I found many still embedded in me where they had lost them. I then took a bird bath from my sink, washing myself with some antibacterial soap, the only form of 'medical attention' I could give myself.

The tier and cells were lethargically cleaned after a few hours. That oxymoron, deafening silence, worked real well to describe the sound of our tier. We were all deeply contemplative men for a while. Only the swish-swish of the broom and the flush of a toilet could be heard.

A couple days later the tractor was gone and a crew had started digging at the entrance to the yellow jacket nest that reached well under the building. I could smell gasoline that they sprayed into it as I watched out the window at their progress. One guy described the hole as being as big as two full-grown men. I shuddered at the thought! They methodically mixed some concrete and poured it into the hole sealing off any wasp recouping of the nest.

The final step in getting the place back to 'normal' was to clean out the ventilation system. A lot of them lay dead in there. Every once in a while the light breeze blowing from one vent would shoot out a wing, and I would just about panic at the sight. Seeing the vacuum truck pull up to clean the vents was sobbingly welcome.

What wasn't welcome was when they snaked the hose in there and started the motor up. Many of us screamed and went into panic attacks at the whining, buzzing sound it made. It was so eerily similar to the wasps we couldn't force our bodies to recognize what our minds know to be only the vacuum and not another invasion of wasps.

Being on death row I frequently deal in ironies. The wasps' needles didn't kill me, but the state has one that does. The prison wasn't concerned with medical treatment, but they love to give out psychotropic drugs. Sphexsophobia – fear of wasps, and anxiety attacks have been diagnosed in virtually everyone. I recently read that yellow jacket venom has proven promising in clinical trials in the treatment of cancer. I may have been inadvertently pretreated for cancer, but the effects won't be of any use because the state has deemed me unworthy to live.

And, who knows, if I could only make it off death row and out of prison, I could become a world-renowned expert of wasps. How's that for irony?

APPENDIX B

JERRY MORRIS

An essay by Harry Joseph Prescott

4 pages, app. 850 words   May 2010

This begins the seventh essay I have written to correspond to the seventh execution since I got here. The killing machine won't stop and shows no sign of slacking up.

When I came to prison in August 1996, the first cell (cell 100) I passed had Marty Nelson in it; cell 99 had James Hollinsworth and cell 98 Jerry Morris. I can still visualize him standing at the door as I go by, a big fat guy with a bald head only acknowledging me by nodding his head. I kept going down the tier to cell 94. Marty and James both escaped execution by getting relief through mental retardation and juvenile issues respectively.

Even though I was just down the tier from Jerry, we never had much conversation. This has been the common theme with all the guys thus far executed. I didn't want to kick it with people, I couldn't become friends or care about because that would only make their deaths more difficult to contend with. Be dispassionate became my rule.

Jerry was from ___ County like I was, and he too had Robert Majors as his trial attorney. My very first rule violation report (RVR) was beating on the iron above my cell door to get medical attention for Big Jerry. (Some called him Ox). He was never a healthy man. Mr. Majors said he was like that when he went to trial in the '80s.

Being unwell never stopped him from smashing lots of food. He had this long rope hooked up so that when guys ate what they wanted off their trays, he would toss the end down the tier and as he pulled it back by each cell they would stack their trays on top of it. He could put away huge amounts of food and it didn't matter what.

He was a quiet man the time I was around him which turned out to be little because in 1997 there was a protest to get the smokes back that I participated in and he did not. He was moved off the tier and I can't recall if we were near one another ever again.

Standard operating procedure here is that once an execution date has been set that person gets moved to a front observation cell. Ironically enough this is so the tower officer can monitor them so that they don't hurt themselves. The prison wants that privilege all its own.

On ____ the prison moved Big Jerry and Jim Bob Butler to those front cells. Jerry's date was May 19th and Jim Bob's was May 20th. I saw Jerry one time in that cell but did not speak.

He stayed there until May 17. That evening the warden and some K-9 officers came to collect him and his property. They transported him to ____ an empty unit where the execution would be carried out.

Tuesday the tier was quieter than normal. We were pretty much lost in our thoughts. I tried to sleep away many of the hours. At 6 p.m. the prison went on lockdown; the only reason they let us out of our cells was a few minutes to get a shower, both Wednesday and Thursday.

Wednesday was a horribly beautiful day. The sun was bright, the sky clear, a warm breeze coming in the window, and it was a glaring contrast to what was soon to come.

As each hour ticked away, I kept thinking that they would call it off. Hoping! This is insane; stop killing people! At four I was thinking he has only two hours left, one hour, 30 minutes. But my mind really scared me when it kept exchanging the pronouns: not he, but I, have two hours, one hour, 30 minutes left. Each execution makes my own all the more probable. Good God, I don't want to die!

The news described a predictably large last meal of hamburgers, onion rings, ice cream, and root beer. It also reported that he had no family present and that there were no protesters. That made it all the more tragic to die at the hands of the state and no one cares.

He was given 15 minutes to make a statement. He recited the Lord's Prayer and asked for forgiveness. This made me think of a filibuster – talk your heart out, postpone death as long as you can, because as soon as you stop talking they will kill you. But it didn't matter if he talked on and on – they just cut the mike off and went to work pushing those lethal chemicals into his veins.

He was pronounced at 6:39 p.m. He asked that his body be released to the University Medical Center in ____. Some medical students will continue the tradition of learning dissection with a criminal's body.

APPENDIX C

JIM BOB BUTLER

An essay by Harry Joseph Prescott

3 pages, app. 730 words   May 2010

The first back-to-back executions since I got here, Big Jerry on May 19 and Jim Bob on May 20. This killing machine has sputtered over the years, but I believe that it will steamroll a lot of us in the next couple.

Jim Bob was the oldest person on the row at 72, but wasn't the oldest to be executed. Mr. Nickerson still holds that title, and he was 77.

I had a little interaction with Jim Bob, but the few conversations we had quickly showed me he was not the kind of person I wanted to do my time around.

One of the most troubling discussions I had with him was about the Bible. He argued that the one people read today was not the real one. The one his daddy had was a huge tome about 6 or 7 inches thick. According to Jim Bob, the real Bible explicitly explained that white people were the chosen ones, and that white supremacy was God's will.

It is a usual practice here that cell neighbors share with one another. Each associates more with the person next door than, say, someone on the opposite end of the tier. With Jim Bob beside me, I had no problem sharing my smokes and coffee. But when mine ran out, he had no talk for me. And when he had some, he never had enough to share. Situations like that taught me a lot of how people operate; they made me deal with fewer people each year.

Thankfully I have long given up smoking, but I am hard-core coffee addict.

On April 21, he was moved to a front cell at the same time Big Jerry was. He stayed there until May 18, when he got transported to ____where Jerry was waiting.

This had to be a massive dose of anxiety for Jim Bob. He knew he would already get killed, but he was there for the before and after of killing Jerry. I kept having the image in my mind that Jerry walks by Jim Bob's cell and then is wheeled on a sheet-draped stretcher back by.

His last meal was a 14-oz T-bone steak, baked potato, salad and apple pie. It made me think pedestrian; it reminded me of a family night out at a Mexican restaurant. Not a Taco Bell but a real Mexican place. I ordered a hamburger. My dad was mad we came to a Mexican place, and I don't sample genuine Mexican cuisine.

All that's to say, it's your last meal and you're not going to experiment? What I want to order I don't believe anyone else will.

Jim Bob's hours are winding down and then the news has _____ going ballistic. Two cops dead, two more wounded. The day before was a stark contrast of realities: Jim Bob dying and the cops shooting it out only exemplified this world is going to the dogs.

He is strapped down and hooked up to the needles and then is given his last 15 minutes to speak. He recites Psalms 23, asks for forgiveness and says he's sorry.

I wonder about the guy's last actions being relayed through some reporters. ____ _of CBS is sad that both Jerry and Jim Bob did not look worried. He saw neither execution. Subjective reporting from a non-witness. I wonder if either were given valium – relaxed but still very much aware that they were going to die.

There were apparently three protesters. ____ said they were not causing a ruckus. He made it sound like he expected it of them. Of course, demonize people that don't believe in state-sanctioned murder.

Jim Bob was pronounced at 6:14 p.m. I guess he didn't talk the whole 15 minutes like Jerry, because there is a 25-minute difference between them. He asked that____ conduct the burial, so he never left the prison grounds – never will.

I learned that it cost $11,000 to conduct one execution and 88 personnel. It would seem that executions are recession-proof too.

Printed in the United States
By Bookmasters